Golf

BRUCE FOSSUM

Assistant Professor of Health,
Physical Education, and Recreation;
Golf Coach,
Michigan State University

MARY DAGRAEDT

Associate Professor of Health,
Physical Education, and Recreation;
Golf Coach,
Miami-Dade Junior College;
Ladies Professional Golf
Association, Teaching Member

ALLYN AND BACON, Inc.   **Boston**

Library of Congress Catalog Card Number:
69–17381

Printed in the United States of America.

Cover photograph courtesy of Hillerich & Bradsby Co.,
Louisville, Ky.

Foreword

SPORTS AND OTHER forms of physical activity are an important part of our culture. Recognizing this, Allyn and Bacon has published this distinctive series of books on the basic concepts of a number of physical activities. These books represent a high point in both curriculum design and instructional materials.

The *conceptual approach* has been used in the development of these books. This approach starts with the identification of the *key concepts* around which the activity is structured. These statements, and the sub-concepts which support them, serve as the basis for organizing and relating the facts and skills of the activity into a meaningful whole. The learner is guided in developing these cognitive and motor concepts through a series of *learning experiences*. These experiences are designed to involve him in the learning process, both intellectually and physically. Each experience leads the learner to develop some specific behavior. At the end of each key concept a list of these behaviors (*outcomes*) is given to enable the student to determine if he is learning. If he can demonstrate he has achieved these outcomes, he can be confident that he has conceptualized the material and should be able to perform the activity with some degree of proficiency.

Although these books are designed primarily to be used as supplements to instructional classes, their unique structure and clear presentation can enable a student to learn the activity even without the direction of a teacher if necessary.

The authors have been selected on a national scale. All have excellent backgrounds as performers and teachers in their fields. The combination of these high calibre people and the conceptual organization of the material has produced a series of books which will be of great value in improving instruction in physical education.

Thomas W. Evaul, Temple University
Raymond A. Snyder, University of California

iii

Preface

THIS BOOK HAS been written and constructed with one major purpose in mind: to make the learning of golf both easier and enjoyable for all. The style in which it is written will make the reader not just think—but *do!!* The build-up to action will be concise, so that the reader can get a club in his hand and go to work. In Concepts III and V the authors have used the personal approach in talking directly to the student, making it seem like a private lesson on the practice tee. Concept VI is unique insofar as the learning of golf rules is concerned. The organization of the breaches of the rules according to penalties will facilitate the reader's retention of these rules. In each concept, wherever possible, the logical sequence from tee to green has been followed, also making the material easier to comprehend. *Action* is the byword in most areas, with a compact explanation of all the other areas involved in playing golf interspersed throughout.

Acknowledgments are made to the many students whom the authors have had the privilege of teaching. While instructing them, they were able to experiment with various methods of teaching, thus providing learning experiences for themselves. Appreciation is also extended to their employers, who gave them the opportunity to practice their teaching skills. Special recognition is given to Lewanne Fenty and Mary Fossum, who served as typists, proofreaders and research assistants.

A debt of gratitude is owed Marilynn Smith for her encouragement and assistance. Appreciation is extended to Miss Smith and Bruce Fleisher, who performed for the photographs used in the text, and to Harry Terry, who photographed them. Acknowledgment is also made to A. G. Spalding & Bros., Inc. for many of the photographs used in this book.

Appreciation is extended to the members of the staff of the National Golf Foundation for the statistics on the growth of golf which they supplied the authors. Recognition is also given to Donald Boyd of the Club Shop Inc., Hollywood, Florida for the information regarding the construction of clubs, the selection of clubs to fit the individual and their maintenance.

The authors of this book have been successful in teaching thousands of men and women of all ages, in numerous settings, to enjoy the game of golf. Each is a college golf coach, a physical education teacher and a golf professional. In addition, they both travel around the United States serving as master clinicians in golf for the Lifetime Sports Education Project sponsored by the American Association for Health, Physical Education, and Recreation, as well as serving as teaching consultants in numerous golf projects and for golf equipment companies.

Bruce Fossum
Mary Dagraedt

Contents

Concept I—Golf, the Sport of a Lifetime, Has Enjoyed an Exciting Development in Becoming One of the Most Popular Sports in the World Today

GOLF, A UNIVERSAL sport, is played by millions of people of all ages in every walk of life. Statistics compiled by the National Golf Foundation show that golf is the fastest growing competitive sport in our nation today.

Items such as golf equipment and attire have undergone change, adding to the enjoyment and comfort of its participants. The enormous growth in competitive events from the community to the national level has been instrumental in forcing additions and clarifications of the rules and standards of procedures governing the game. Various organizations have sprung up to supply the leadership needed for the numerous aspects of the sport.

1. The object of the game of golf is to complete the round in the fewest strokes possible, while stroking the ball from the tee to the green with a variety of clubs.

A round of golf usually consists of 18 holes, although any number of holes may be played. Starting from the teeing ground of the first hole, generally located near the club house or professional shop, you may elevate your ball from the ground by using a small object called a *tee*. You are permitted to use a tee only when *teeing-off* at each hole, after which you play the ball as it lies. Continue to stroke the ball each time it is your turn until it enters the hole of the putting green being played. Your overall goal is to complete each hole and the entire round in the fewest possible strokes.

The drawing shown is of a hole with a *dogleg* (turn in the fairway) to the left. Located on the teeing ground are three sets of markers. The markers farthest from the hole are generally used by expert players, the ones next farthest are used by the less expert men players, while the most forward markers are for women. Included in the drawing are hazards such as a lateral

1

A Typical Hole

water hazard (running parallel to the fairway), a direct water hazard (running perpendicular to the fairway), a fairway bunker (sand trap) and several bunkers surrounding the green. The architect makes strategic use of the natural topography to make a course interesting and challenging. Often these hazards are planned so as to penalize poorly executed shots. Out-of-bounds markers (stakes, walls or fence posts) are placed to indicate the outside boundaries of the course. Some courses also employ out-of-bounds markers on the inside boundaries of the course. This local adjustment helps to discourage a player from deliberately cutting across a dogleg to an adjacent fairway to shorten the overall length of a hole, lessening the danger to the group proceeding down this fairway. The *fairway* (mowed terrain leading from the tee to the green), usually from 30 to 60 yards wide, is bordered by *rough* (longer grass) often interspersed with bushes, trees and other natural growing objects. Immediately next to the green is a closely cut portion of the fairway called the *apron*. The *putting green* is the rug-like area on which the *flagstick*, which bears the number of the hole on a pennant, is sunk in a 4¼″ hole.

A golfer's dream is to shoot par or sub-par golf. *Par* is the number of strokes it takes an expert player to play the hole. In computing par, two putts are allowed on each hole besides the number of strokes it should take the expert player to reach the green. Par is set up according to the following chart, although the difficulty of the hole may alter the par.

PAR COMPUTATIONS		
Par	*Yardages for Men*	*Yardages for Women*
3	up to 250	up to 210
4	251–470	211–400
5	471 up	401–575
6		576 up

Par Computation Chart

A score of one under par is called a *birdie*, while a score of two under par is called an *eagle*. An *ace* or a *hole-in-one* may be made by hitting the ball from the tee into the hole in one stroke. One over par is called a *bogey*, while two over par is referred to as a *double bogey*.

After completing each hole, the scorer should mark the scores made on the scorecard *immediately upon reaching the next tee*. A sample scorecard is shown below. Note that the yardage, par and handicap rating for each hole appears on the scorecard.

The USGA has devised a system of handicapping which allows all golfers, regardless of their ability, a chance to compete on equal terms with each other. A booklet, "Golf Committee Manual and USGA Golf Handicap System," gives complete information about the handicapping system and the course rating system.

A handicap chairman, who is provided with all the information regarding handicapping, computes each club member's handicap. The handicap is posted where it may be found readily. When playing a match using handicaps, subtract the difference between your opponent's handicap and your own. If your handicap is two strokes higher than your opponent's, he must give you a stroke on the holes listed as 1 (hole 4) and 2 (hole 14) in the handicap rating column. The handicap hole rated 1 is the hole on the first nine on which the entire membership averages the highest score. The handicap hole rated 2 is the hole on the second nine on which these players average the highest score.

LEARNING EXPERIENCE—HANDICAP HOLES
Examine the scorecard shown and determine on which holes a player would be given a stroke if a total of five strokes were given him in match play.

When playing stroke play for low net in a tournament, a player's handicap is subtracted from his *gross score* (score actually shot) to get his *net score* (actual score less handicap).

Often participants who wish to enter a one-day handicap tournament do not have an established handicap. The *Callaway Handicap System* is a system of handicapping which determines a player's handicap based on his 18-hole score. The system can

SPRING CREEK GOLF COURSE

HOLE	1	2	3	4	5	6	7	8	9	OUT	10	11	12	13	14	15	16	17	18	IN	TOTAL	HDCP.	NET
CHAMPIONSHIP	435	415	199	443	526	429	125	384	559	3515	395	425	525	213	445	347	536	175	463	3524	7039		
REGULAR	409	397	170	412	503	403	113	361	526	3294	363	389	494	178	386	323	507	147	425	3212	6506		
LADIES	360	335	139	338	401	352	95	336	490	2844	331	352	460	127	323	297	407	123	378	2798	5642		
PAR	4	4	3	4	5	4	3	4	5	36	4	4	5	3	4	4	5	3	4	36	72		
HDCP. RATING	3	11	15	1	7	9	17	13	5		12	4	8	14	2	16	10	18	6				

SCORER _____

ATTEST _____

DATE _____

U.S.G.A. Rules Govern Play

Sample Scorecard

be found in the booklet "Competitive Golf Events," published by the National Golf Foundation.

2. The ability to become skillful in golf, although it adds to the enjoyment of the game, does not detract from the numerous values received from the sport.

People of all ages and with different physical aptitudes play golf for a variety of reasons. Although one may learn to play the game of golf more readily when he is 10 to 12 years old, it is never too late to start golfing. Many people take up golf after they retire. A younger person who is more supple may be able to pivot better and employ a longer, faster swing, thus getting greater distance than an older person. A taller person, who has a longer swing arc, has an advantage in distance potential. Arm and wrist strength, along with good timing, are other factors important to achieving distance. Most women cannot hit the ball as far as men due to this lack of strength. A calm, even-tempered individual will not be as apt to lose control of his reasoning power and will have a greater chance to shoot a steady game than an ill-tempered person. A feeling of confidence is a real attribute. It is often stated that the game of golf is 40% psychological. If this is true, a person who cannot control his temper or who is insecure will have only a limited chance for success.

To achieve the status of a par golfer requires much time for both practice and play. Many top amateurs and professionals, when not involved in a tournament, practice from four to six hours a day and play at least five times a week. The Sunday golfer should not expect to shoot par golf but should be satisfied with other outcomes and values.

Golf's health benefits cannot be overlooked. The chance to be out of doors and to get some exercise, while enjoying the beauty of nature, is a joy for many confined to indoor work. The sport can be as strenuous as the individual wishes it to be, for he may set his own pace. He may walk carrying his bag, or pull a cart with or without a motor. He may employ a caddy to carry his bag while he walks, or he may choose to ride in a motorized cart. He may also select the number of holes to be played, according to his physical endurance and the amount of leisure time he enjoys. Because of these adaptations many seriously ill and physically handicapped individuals may still enjoy the game of golf. Wheel chair golf is not uncommon, particularly on the short "par 3" courses.

Many therapeutic benefits are derived from the game. Aggressions are often relieved through hitting the ball. Pressures at the office are often forgotten in the beautiful settings. Industry, recognizing the many benefits to be derived from the game, has formed leagues for its employees and in many cases has even built courses for them. The improvement in employee morale has justified this expenditure.

For many, golf is a business asset. Many business deals have been negotiated on a golf course. Many employers take potential employees to the golf course for an interview whereby they may ascertain such characteristics as self-control, honesty, sportsmanship and courtesy.

Men and women may enjoy the game of golf together. It is one of the few games in which people of unequal ability can find pleasure in one another's company, since in most cases each is playing his own game independently of the others in his group. It is a particular pleasure to observe a family playing together.

Golf, once considered to be a rich man's game, may now be enjoyed by people from all income brackets. The cost of the equipment is no longer prohibitive and there are numerous courses in existence today whose green fees and memberships are in the reach of almost any budget.

Golf, without a doubt, is a lifetime sport which helps you to stay physically fit. It allows you the joy of meeting people and socializing while relaxing and having fun in the outdoors.

Outcomes

After this introduction to the game of golf, you should be able to:
1. Name and describe all of the areas and items which may be present on any golf hole.
2. Explain the basis on which the par for a given hole is computed for both men and women.
3. Discuss what is meant by the terms *low gross* and *low net*.
4. List at least ten values which may be derived from playing golf.

Concept II—The Necessity to Carefully Select, Care for and Maintain Essential Golf Equipment Cannot Be Overemphasized

THE ADVICE OF a competent instructor or golf professional should be sought when one plans to buy golf equipment, just as the advice of a physician should be obtained before a person in ill health purchases medicine. Too often the beginner chooses equipment which does not suit him, even though it is easier to buy a set of suitable golf clubs than it is to buy a suit of clothes. Approximately ninety percent of all golfers can be properly equipped with a standard model from almost any leading manufacturer. Even the beginner should understand the basic facts about golf clubs so that he can discuss his needs intelligently when purchasing a set of clubs. He should also be aware that clubs with changeable faces (*lofts*) are illegal, as are clubs with hollowed grips to help him achieve the correct grip. Once a suitable set of clubs is purchased, a small amount of care will help preserve it. Normally when we speak of golf equipment we think of golf clubs. Technically, however, equipment includes anything the player wears, carries or has carried for him, except the ball he is playing.

1. A beginning golfer can achieve a reasonable amount of success with a minimum of six clubs.

When you first decide to take up the game of golf, it is often recommended that you buy a good second-hand set of clubs which will be usable while you develop your swing, rather than a new set of inexpensive clubs of inferior quality. After you have developed a swing, a professional will be able to help you select a suitable set of clubs. If you buy new clubs, buy a standard brand. You will later be able to replace a lost club or complete the set if you are unable to purchase an entire matched set at once. The four irons (3–5–7–9), putter and 3-wood make up the minimum number of clubs recommended for good play. A driver would logically be the next club to add. Although the rules of golf permit you to carry a maximum of 14 clubs, you can enjoy the game with far fewer clubs. Nevertheless, you should be familiar with all of the clubs and their uses.

A Matched Set of Clubs (Courtesy of A. G. Spalding & Bros., Inc.; Photograph by Harry Terry)

The above photograph shows a matched set of clubs (L to R) containing a number 1 (driver), number 3 (spoon), number 4 (cleek) and number 5 wood. The driver has the longest shaft and the least angled face. As the numbers of the woods increase, their shafts are graduated approximately one half inch shorter and the loft of their faces increases. Thus a ball hit with a 4 wood will travel higher and less far than a ball hit with a 3 wood. The set of irons shown contains the 3, 4, 5, 6, 7, 8 and 9 irons, pitching wedge, sand wedge and putter. Again, the smaller the number, the longer the shaft and the less lofted the face of the club. Some people include a 2 iron, 2 wood (*brassie*) or some other club instead of one of the clubs above. It is up to you which combination of clubs you wish to use, as long as the total number does not exceed the 14-club maximum.

The next two drawings show the loft of a standard man's set of woods and irons and the approximate distance a man of average ability might expect to hit the ball with each club. His club selection for a particular shot will be determined primarily by the loft he desires and the distance he wishes the ball to travel. The primary use of the sand wedge is to get out of a bunker, while the putter is used on the green to putt the ball into the hole. Club selection for the basic and advanced shots of golf will be discussed later.

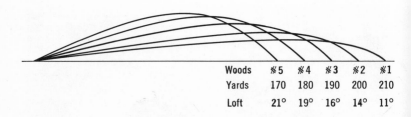

Woods	#5	#4	#3	#2	#1
Yards	170	180	190	200	210
Loft	21°	19°	16°	14°	11°

Average Loft of Woods

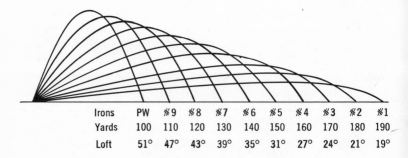

Irons	PW	#9	#8	#7	#6	#5	#4	#3	#2	#1
Yards	100	110	120	130	140	150	160	170	180	190
Loft	51°	47°	43°	39°	35°	31°	27°	24°	21°	19°

Average Loft of Irons

If a player hits the ball well, it can be assumed that there will be approximately a 10-yard difference in distance with each club used. If he hits a 5 iron 150 yards, then he can expect to hit a 4 iron 160 yards and a 6 iron 140 yards.

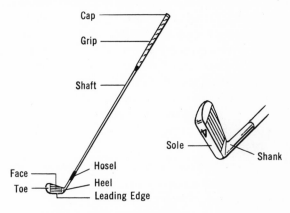

Parts of a Golf Club

Become familiar with your golf clubs so you will understand the terminology used when the skills of the game are presented.

2. Some of the more important items which should be considered when selecting a set of clubs include the size of the grip, the swing weight, overall weight, shaft flexibility and length.

A golf professional will discuss the five points mentioned above, and perhaps the loft and the lie of your club, when he helps you select a set of clubs. Although the "feel" may be the final word in the selection, the following items should be considered:

SIZE OF THE GRIP. The length of your fingers, rather than the overall size of your hand, is the important factor when deciding whether a $\frac{1}{32}$-inch undersize grip or a $\frac{1}{32}$- or $\frac{1}{16}$-inch oversize grip is preferable to the standard grip. Again, "feel" will be a factor.

SWINGWEIGHT. Swingweight denotes the proportion of the weight in the head of the club to the weight of the shaft and the grip. As the clubs get shorter their heads get heavier, so they will swing the same way. The addition of three paper dollar bills on the head of a D-0 club will raise it two swingweights to a D-2. Swingweights are referred to by the letters A, B, C, D and E, each letter having gradations from zero through 9. C-4 to C-7 is the swingweight used by most women golfers, although many of the stronger women players select C-8, C-9 or clubs in the D-0 to D-3 category. Most men select a club in the D-1 to D-5 category. A and B swingweights are rare as they are unusually light, while seldom is an E swingweight found in any other club than a sand wedge. The trend is currently toward the use of slightly lighter swingweights so that more clubhead speed can be generated. It is advisable to buy a matched set of clubs from a "pro shop" to ensure that each club will have the same swing-weight (feel). Only then can your timing be developed for "one swing."

OVERALL WEIGHT. There is no need to worry about this aspect of the club, since all reliable companies make the overall weight of the club in proper proportion to the swingweight. The average weight of a man's driver is 13 to 13¼ ounces, while a woman's driver weighs approximately 12¾ ounces. If one is having any adjustments made on his clubs, he should have it done either by the company who made the club or by a knowledgeable club maker. It is only when untrained individuals alter swing-weights, grip size, etc., that the overall weight becomes too light or too heavy, or is in an improper relationship.

SHAFT FLEXIBILITY. The bend or "whip" of the shaft can be described as flexible, medium or stiff. Some companies make clubs with five different flexibilities. The flexible or whippiest shaft is used by most women golfers, and by men who have slow swings. The shaft with a medium amount of flex is used by stronger women players and lighter hitting men. The stiff shafts should be employed only by long-hitting men who are able to play golf at least three or four times a week.

If a player uses a club with a swingweight too light for him and a shaft which is too flexible, he will lose distance and most likely "hook" the ball. If the swingweight is too heavy and the shaft too stiff, he will tend to hit the ball to the right.

LENGTH. The length of club one should use is determined not by his height, but by the strength and the length of his arms. If he is tall with long arms, a standard set of clubs will suit him.

The distance from the fingertips to the ground is the important factor. If the distance is greater than 28 inches, he might prefer clubs longer than standard. Conversely, if the distance is less than 26 inches he might want clubs shorter than standard. A short person who is strong and well coordinated, with fingertips measuring approximately 27 inches from the ground, might add distance to his game by selecting a club with extra length, thus increasing his arc.

3. It is important for all beginning golfers to select suitable golf attire, balls and other necessary accessories.

GOLF ATTIRE. Clothing which allows for freedom of movement is important. Acceptable attire for a man consists of a bermuda short or a pair of slacks with a shirt. A bermuda-length short, culotte, skirt or pair of slacks worn with a blouse is considered proper attire for women. A sport dress may also be worn. Sweaters and rain gear should be carried. A street shoe with a flat heel which offers support is suitable for both men and women. Most beginners need not buy golf shoes immediately, nor need they buy a golf glove unless blisters appear.

BALLS. A high-compression (100) ball which is tightly wound and which has a thin cover is not the ball which should be chosen by the novice. He would rarely hit it hard enough to compress it sufficiently to get distance. Thus he would be better off to buy a lower-compression (80–90), less tightly wound ball with a more durable cover which will respond to a weaker hit, yet will not cut so readily. Low-compression balls can be bought cheaply. In cold weather, even a skilled player often discards the high-compression ball due to the difficulty encountered in compressing it in this type of weather.

BAG. A light inexpensive "Sunday" bag will be suitable for the beginning golfer. It is light enough to be carried, thus alleviating the need for a golf cart or caddy, yet has sufficient room for the essential items such as tees, balls, etc.

4. A small amount of care will help to preserve the life of your equipment.

Head covers should be used to cover the woods to keep them from getting nicked.

Your clubs should be cleaned each time they are used. The grooves in the faces of the clubs should not be allowed to become clogged with dirt, as little spin can be attained if the grooves are filled. Rubber grips may be washed with soap and water, while saddle soap should be used on leather grips.

Irons may be soaked in water containing a detergent. A stiff brush may be used to remove the dirt from the grooves, after which the irons should be dried thoroughly. A light coat of machine or similar oil should be used to keep them from rusting. If a silicone cloth is used on the heads of the irons, care should be exercised to keep the cloth away from the grips.

Woods should never be soaked in water. Use as little water as practicable, on a damp cloth, when wiping off the woods. A stiff-bristled brush (*not* metal bristles) may be used. Be careful not to mar the finish of the wood. Apply a coat of car or furniture polish to the head of the wood. Rub a small amount of linseed oil on the face of the wood about once a month. This replaces the lost moisture in the wood and acts to fill the pore-holes, thus keeping out an excessive amount of water. The wood will turn "whitish" when it is porous and susceptible to water. When this occurs at least the face of the wood should be refinished.

Tighten the screws on the face of the woods periodically. Replace caps, grips and other worn-out parts when it becomes necessary.

Clubs should not be stored in the trunk of a car, as the heat of the trunk steams the clubs if they are damp. They should be stored in a dry area to prevent them from warping and rusting. With just a little care, a set of clubs will last you for a number of years. Your club "pro shop" or local club shop has people qualified to help you keep your clubs in good playing condition.

Outcomes

As a result of studying about the equipment used for golf, its care and maintenance, you should be able to do the following:

1. Name the clubs you should purchase if you are buying the minimum number of clubs for golf.

2. Explain why a standard brand is recommended when purchasing a set of clubs.

3. Describe the difference in the construction of a 2 iron and a 5 iron, and discuss the difference in the flight and carry you should expect with each club.

4. List five important items to consider when selecting a set of clubs, and explain what is meant by each.

5. Discuss what is meant by a matched set of clubs.

6. State what is considered proper golf attire for both men and women.

7. Discuss the various compressions of golf balls, and indicate what kind of golfer should use each type.

8. Explain how to care properly for both your woods and your irons.

Concept III—The Grip, Set Up to the Ball and a Sound Swing Are the Three Most Important Factors in Determining Your Success in the Five Fundamental Skills of the Full Swing, Pitching, Chipping, Hitting Sand Shots and Putting

THE BEST STRIKERS of the golf ball today rely on their ability to follow these concepts carefully as they practice, striving for consistency in all phases. The habits they develop on the practice range evolve into "muscle-memory" and the repeating golf swing which they rely on when playing the game. They are then able to concentrate on the other details necessary to improve their score.*

The material on the skills which follows will be discussed in a personal way: *a teacher-to-student relationship.*

1. The grip taken on a golf club is the most important fundamental in achieving success in golf.

The grip is your only contact with the club! With a club at your disposal, get ready to learn how to hold it correctly! The grip described below is the *"ten-finger grip."*

A) From a normal standing posture, place the sole of the club on the ground (floor), in front of you. Support the club with the right thumb and index finger. The sole should rest on the ground with its leading edge perpendicular (square) to the intended line of flight. The grooves (lines) on the face of the club should be pointing straight ahead.

B) Extend the fingers of the left hand, palm up and fingers together, behind and against the club, with the little finger about

---

* A note to left-handers all over the world, with no disrespect in mind, but only joy that you are playing the game of a lifetime—the descriptions in this text are given from the right-hander's point of view. Do your best to transpose the material to your side of the ball. A mirror will be of great use to you!

one to one-and-one-half inches below the butt end of the grip. The hand should be in a diagonal position, so that the second pad of the index finger and the third pads of the other three fingers will be blocked from your vision by the grip of the club. (See left-hand drawing.)

C) Curl the fingers around the club securely. (See middle drawing.)

D) Fold the thumb and palm over the top of the grip. This secures the left hand correctly on the club. The thumb should be pointing down the shaft, resting a little to the right of center. (See right-hand drawing.)

Checkpoints for the left-hand grip are as follows:

1) In bending slightly from the waist and neck, you should be able to observe two knuckles of the left hand.
2) The apex of the "V" formed by the thumb and index finger should point somewhere between the right ear and the right shoulder.

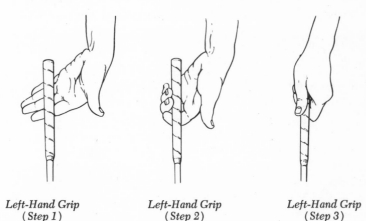

Left-Hand Grip   *Left-Hand Grip*   *Left-Hand Grip*
   (Step 1)   *(Step 2)*   *(Step 3)*

LEARNING EXPERIENCE—CHECK FOR PROPER
LEFT-HAND GRIP
Assume the left-hand grip. Stand in front of a mirror and check the "V" formed by the thumb and index finger. (Remember, the mirror will reverse your position.) Feel the control through your fingers. You will discover that your thumb must be extended down the shaft

*below the line of your index finger (long thumb), in order to achieve
this "feel" through the fingers. If your hand has been placed correctly
on the grip, your thumb will point straight down the shaft and rest
slightly to the right of center.*

E) With your left hand secured on the grip, place your right
hand, fingers extended toward the target, in a position below
the left hand and behind the grip, hiding the second pad of the
index finger and the third pads of the other fingers behind the
grip.

F) Curl the fingers of the right hand around the grip and slide
the whole hand up and against the index finger of the left hand.
(See left-hand drawing.)

G) Fold the thumb and palm over the top of the grip so that
the lifeline of the right hand fits snugly over the thumb of the
left hand.

Checkpoints for the right-hand grip are as follows:

1) The "V" formed by the thumb and index finger points somewhere between the right ear and the right shoulder and paral-
   lels the "V" of the left hand.
2) The right thumb is positioned to the left of the center of the
   grip, pointing down the grip.
3) The thumb of the left hand fits snugly into the lifeline of the
   right hand.

Right-Hand Grip   *"Ten-Finger" Grip*   *"Ten-Finger" Grip*
                              (Complete)   *(Eye View)*

4) The index finger is separated slightly from the rest of the hand, in a "trigger" position. The tip of the index finger will just about touch the tip of the thumb. (See center and right-hand drawings.)

How firmly should you grip the club? Hold the club with just your left hand. Feel secure through the last three fingers: these are the pressure points. There should be a slight firmness in the lower part of the forearm. The left hand is the key control factor in the grip. If it becomes loose, especially at the top of the backswing, control is lost.

LEARNING EXPERIENCE—DEVELOPING STRENGTH IN THE LEFT HAND
Grip the club with just the left hand. Lift the club up and point it directly in front of you. Remove the thumb and index finger. Bounce the club up and down and move it back and forth—feel the control through the last three fingers.

The pressure exerted by the right hand is felt through the middle two fingers, with the overall feeling about half as firm as the left hand. If you feel any tension through the forearm, you are holding the club too tightly. The final act of striking the ball will be delivered by the right hand; therefore the wrist must be quite flexible, yet firm enough through the middle fingers to control the club.

Finally, and most important to the good player, is a feeling of togetherness of the hands. This is felt mainly through the connection of the left thumb and the palm of the right hand and the closeness of both hands on the grip. Some experimenting is necessary to get the proper feeling.

LEARNING EXPERIENCE—PROPER GRIP CHECK
Assume the correct grip. Examine the checkpoints carefully. Check pressure points. Grip for ten seconds, remove hands, grip again. Feel "togetherness" of the hands. Waggle (swing the clubhead back and forth a few inches) the club a few times with just your hands. Feel the grip. Repeat this exercise once more and review the checkpoints again.

Although we have assumed the "ten-finger" grip first, there are two other grips that are used by most advanced players. Most beginners are able to assume the "ten-finger" grip most easily, since it is the grip which feels the most natural to them. It is always possible to change to another grip under the direction of a competent instructor. Size of hands and length of fingers determine the grip which is best suited for you. The grip that gives you the best control should be the grip for you to adopt.

THE OVERLAPPING OR VARDON GRIP. This grip is accepted by the majority of teachers and used by most experts. It places the hands in a position of comfortable "togetherness." Most experts have strong hands and forearms and have discovered through experience that the "ten-finger" grip is dominated too much by the right hand. This takes away the "togetherness" of the hands, a feeling essential in executing consistent golf shots. If your game and score indicate a change in grip is necessary, or if your instructor suggests a change, it would be wise to investigate the possibilities of the overlapping grip. In this grip, note that one finger of the right hand (the little finger) is removed from the grip and curled comfortably over the left index finger, allowing the hands to be very close together. (See the illustrations.)

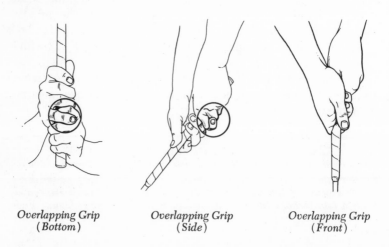

| Overlapping Grip | Overlapping Grip | Overlapping Grip |
| (Bottom) | (Side) | (Front) |

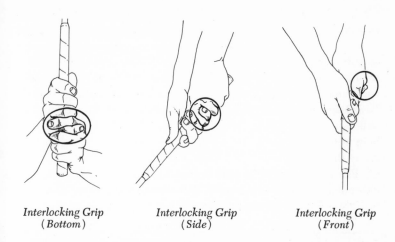

Interlocking Grip   Interlocking Grip   Interlocking Grip
   (Bottom)   (Side)   (Front)

THE INTERLOCKING GRIP. The interlocking grip is also an alteration of the "ten-finger" grip. This grip allows for the removal of two fingers from the grip. The little finger of the right hand is entwined with the index finger of the left hand. This places the hands in a very close position, and the "marriage" has been found most acceptable by many fine players. Again, your instructor can help you decide whether or not this grip is right for you. (See the illustrations.) The checkpoints for this grip, as well as the overlapping grip, are identical to those of the "ten-finger" grip. Never allow yourself to forget that *your hands are the only connection between you and the clubhead.* They are the key control factors in swinging the club and striking the ball. A correct grip cannot be overemphasized as the most important basic in golf.

2. A proper stance and a consistent relationship to the ball must be assumed prior to striking a golf ball.

You cannot expect to swing a golf club acceptably without proper preparation. Assuming a correct stance will place you in a proper physical position that will enable you to strike the ball as well as you can within your physical potential.

Follow the suggestions and checkpoints listed on page 22:

A) Stand with your feet turned slightly outward. Your feet should be about shoulder width apart for a normal wood or long iron shot. They will be a little closer together when swinging a medium or short iron.

B) Flex your knees as if you are *starting* to "sit down." Squeeze your knees inward so that you feel you are standing slightly "knock-kneed." You will find that the greater amount of weight will fall on the inside borders of your feet. This position will help you set up for a proper turning action once you begin to swing the club.

C) Bend from the waist only far enough to sole the club on the ground. Make sure the clubhead is square to the intended line of flight. (See left-hand and center illustrations.)

LEARNING EXPERIENCE—PROPER WIDTH OF THE STANCE
For the correct width of the feet, you can plumbline with the use of a club. Use a mirror. Hold the grip end of the club at the point of either shoulder and bend slightly from the waist. Allow the club to hang straight down. It should point to the instep of the foot. Double-check this from the point of both shoulders.

D) The left arm should be extended but not tense or stiff. It should be in a straight line with the club.

E) To set up consistent ball position with all clubs—and, more important, to set you the right distance from the ball—make sure that your left knee cap is covered from your vision by your left wrist. Simply, "left wrist covers left knee cap."

F) Your right elbow should point at the crest of your right hip. (Elbow will remain pointing at the hip throughout the golf swing.)

G) Your weight is balanced between the feet and over the arches of each foot.

LEARNING EXPERIENCE—CHECK FOR PROPER STANCE
Use the "buddy" system. Examine one another's stance, using the checkpoints of the stance. Assume stance, observe, relax; reassume stance, observe, relax.

Stance (Frontal)   Stance (Behind, look-   Assuming Square
                          ing toward target)   Stance with Use
                                                        of "H."

Now that you have assumed a correct and acceptable posture,
let us continue with the *proper relationship to the ball and alignment* to your intended line of flight.

Lay a club on the ground pointing directly toward your
target. Now, assume a proper stance with both your toes just
touching the shaft of the club. This places your feet in what is
called a "square" position. Your knees, hips and shoulders should
follow this pattern. Your right shoulder will be lower than your
left, due to the fact that your right hand is lower on the club
than the left. This set-up over the ball is called the "square"
stance. Use this stance for all normal, full golf shots. Other
stances will be discussed later. In the position just described, lay
another club at right angle to the first so that its line is just inside the left heel. Your ball will be placed somewhere on the
line of this club, depending on the length club you use for a
given shot. Take a club in your hand and set up using the square
stance. Sole your club just behind the club placed by the left
instep. Place another club on the ground at exactly the point
where your clubhead is soled and point it at the target (right-
hand illustration). The "H" formed by the three clubs will help
you achieve a square stance, proper ball position, alignment to
the target and line of flight for the shot. Practice setting up using

this method. It is sound procedure to do this for self-analysis any time you are practicing.

Ball position for a normal golf shot is always relative to the left heel. Later, as you learn different shots with various clubs, your stance may change in width or direction, but your ball position will remain consistent for normal shots.

Let us examine the final steps in assuming a proper stance, removing the guidelines. Here is an accepted method that you can practice:

1) Stand behind the ball and visualize the line of your intended shot. 2) Sole your club squarely behind the ball, semi-facing your target (left-hand drawing). 3) Step into address position now. By soling the club first, you have determined approximately how far you must stand away from the ball. Place your feet together and have the ball placed directly off the line of the *right* foot (center drawing). 4) Move your right foot away from the target until it is approximately shoulder width. Make minor adjustments for comfort and alignment (right-hand drawing).

As you progress in the game, you will develop your own style in setting up properly; at this time the above procedure is recommended.

Assuming Stance
(Step 1)

Assuming Stance
(Step 2)

Assuming Stance
(Step 3)

LEARNING EXPERIENCE—ASSUMING A PROPER STANCE
Set the clubs on the ground in the "H" pattern described. Assume a

proper stance. Check your grip. Examine all checkpoints of the stance and make sure they are correct. Step away and repeat. Check your balance. Remove the clubs and, using the method described with the guidelines removed, practice setting up without help. Get the feel of it. Do this several times. You will find that it sets you up quickly and accurately.

---

3. The full swing is a fine combination of timing and balance.

What strikes the ball? After very little thought, you will arrive at the conclusion that it is the face of the clubhead. How does the clubhead arrive at this position? *By swinging the club.* Power is developed from clubhead speed. Direction comes from body control. Both are developed through good *balance* and *timing*. You have a good foundation now that you have learned to grip the club correctly and set up to the ball in good posture and balance. Balance can be described in a negative way: when you are out of balance, you are out of control. Timing is another thing. Establish a rhythm to your swing, a tempo or a beat by which you can swing the clubhead according to your own make-up. Once you begin swinging, your own timing will develop. It might be well to point out that most golfers swing the club too fast, especially in the vital backswing. With this bit of perspective in mind, let's progress into the elements of a good swing.

A) *GETTING SET TO STRIKE THE BALL.* Once you have established a good grip and proper stance, you should have the feeling of being slightly in motion. Waggle the club a bit as you set your stance. Stay in motion so you will not have a tendency to tighten up over the ball. Many fine players initiate their backswing by using the "forward press," a slight movement of the hands and the right side of the body toward the target. There are many other ways to get started properly. If you keep the idea of "motion" foremost in your mind, you will be off to a good start.

B) *THE BACKSWING.* The experts sometimes refer to this part of the swing as the "moment of truth."

1) Start the backswing with a push from the left side (shoulder, arm, hands and clubhead all together). Keep the club low to

the ground as far as possible. The firmness set up by a good left-hand grip will cause a feeling of unity from the shoulder to the clubhead.

2) Turn the left shoulder *under* the chin until the left hand is just past the left knee. Arm and club are still in line. (See left-hand top drawing.)

3) Now, continue turning the shoulder *under* the chin and raising your arms until the club points in the general direction of the target. Your hands will cock in a very natural way if your grip is correct. (See top center drawing.)

C) *AT THE TOP OF THE BACKSWING.* If you stop in the position just described there are five checkpoints that you can observe:

1) The left arm is still extended. Arms are still close together as in address.

2) The right elbow points at the right hip, with the right hand in a "waiter's" position (carrying a tray).

3) The grip remains the same.

4) Your back should be facing the target.

5) The club should point approximately at the target. (See top center drawing.)

D) *THE DOWNSWING* (Striking the ball). From the "top" position, PULL the club from the whole left side (left shoulder, arm, hand and hip), *down and through* the ball and at the target, keeping your head steady in its original position, behind the ball. (See drawings at top right and at bottom.)

E) *THE FINISH* (Follow-through). Because of a strong *pulling* action *through* the ball, the transfer of weight to the left side and follow-through will be automatic—the *results* of a good swing, not causes. If the *pull* through the ball has been made with good balance and with some vigor, the clubhead will accelerate and you will finish with your hands high, above and slightly to the left of your head. Your hips and upper body will be facing the target. (See drawing at bottom right.)

LEARNING EXPERIENCE—INITIAL MOVEMENT OF DOWNSWING

From the top of the backswing, initiate the downswing by pulling from the left side and stop when your club is horizontal before your hands begin to uncock. Repeat this ten times. Check to see if your weight has begun to transfer to the left side. Is your head steady behind the ball?

Full Swing (1)   Full Swing (2)   Full Swing (3)

Full Swing (4)   Full Swing (5)   Full Swing (6)

There are several exercises which will help you develop your golf swing. Exercises are often executed in retrospect, and a lack of concentration often prevails. Exercise can then be harmful. Remind yourself to concentrate on good posture and proper swing technique while performing each one. Use your regular checkpoints for a good stance and swing as you execute each drill. Keep the objectives in mind as you work—a better golf swing, a better score and more fun.

Swing Drill 1
(Position 1)

Swing Drill 1
(Position 2)

Swing Drill 1
(Position 3)

SWING DRILL #1. From the position shown, turn your shoulder under the chin until the left end of the club points down to the imaginary position of the ball. Now, *pull* from the left side until the right end of the club points down just behind the imaginary position of the ball. Move your left side toward the target. Your head remains steady.

Swing Drill 2
(Position 1)

Swing Drill 2
(Position 2)

Swing Drill 2
(Position 3)

SWING DRILL #2. Concentrate on a good shoulder turn and a strong left arm in this drill. You must push, then pull, the club with good control. Start slowly, then speed up, without losing control.

Swing Drill 3   Swing Drill 3   Swing Drill 3
(Position 1)   (Position 2)   (Position 3)

SWING DRILL #3. Use your regular swing tempo from this position. You will find that it is easier to develop rhythm and a sense of timing with your hands separated.

LEARNING EXPERIENCE—SWINGING THE CLUB

Try each swing drill five times. Observe checkpoints. Next, assume a good stance with both hands correctly on the club. Go through the swing in slow motion about five times. Again observe the checkpoints. Speed up the tempo—with control. Stay in balance and feel the club-head swing. Check your head position throughout the swing by using a full-length mirror. Place a piece of tape on the mirror over the image of your forehead. Try to keep your head steady until your right shoulder begins to push it out of the way. Doing this keeps you over the ball and in good balance.

Now that you are off and swinging, let us begin to adapt that swing to the various clubs which are needed to play the game. We will discuss only the essential shots, covering the more advanced skills later in the text. Most full shots, regardless of the

club used, are executed in much the same way. Minor adjustments will be made for the usage of the different clubs, due only
to the length and loft of the club, the lie of the ball and the
expected results of the shot. What you may reasonably expect
from each club in your bag can only be determined through
practice and experience. In any case, have patience as you learn
and do not expect miracles overnight.

A) *THE TEE SHOT.* You have already learned the difference
between 3-, 4- and 5-par holes. On *most* 4- and 5-par holes, it is
essential that you use a 1-wood (driver) from the teeing ground
for maximum distance. However, until you have learned to use
this club with adequate results, it is better to try the more lofted
3-wood. If you swing well with this club, it will be easier to get
the ball airborne and keep it in play on the fairway.

On 3-par holes, depending on the yardage, you may be required to use almost any club in your bag. Whatever the case, on
the teeing ground you are allowed to place your ball on a tee.
This is an advantage allowed by the rules of golf—use it!

How do you tee the ball? When using the 1-wood, the ball
should be teed approximately one inch above the ground. With
a more lofted wood or with any iron, tee the ball lower. Make it
look like it is setting on *top* of the grass—a perfect lie.

As you practice with your 1-wood, try to keep the following
ideas in mind: 1) Widen the stance two or three inches from
the basic stance. The longer club will command a fuller radius
and arc to your swing, thus demanding a wider base for better
balance. 2) The length of the club will place you further from
the ball but this will not change the checkpoints for a proper
stance. You might try moving your hands away from the target
an inch or two. This will set up more of a *sweeping* motion in the
hitting area, rather than a down-and-through motion of the clubhead. 3) Most beginners make the obvious mistake of swinging
too hard when they use the 1-wood. Strive for control through
timing and good balance.

B) *FULL SHOTS FROM THE FAIRWAY WITH A FAIR-
WAY WOOD (3-, 4- or 5-wood) OR AN IRON.* When
maximum distance is required either to get on the green or get
into position in front of a green, a fairway wood is your best
choice. This wood is designed with enough loft to get the ball

FULL SWING—Marilynn Smith (Courtesy of A. G. Spalding & Bros., Inc.;
Photographs by Harry Terry)

airborne from a good lie, and will give you maximum distance. Assume a normal stance and grip and *sweep* the clubhead through the shot. Let the loft of the club get the ball up and on its way to the target. This is a much used and proficient weapon, especially for women, and much practice with it is advised.

The use of the long and medium irons (2-, 3-, 4-, 5-, 6- and 7-irons) demands no radical change, just a solid reminder to swing the club! Swing the club in good balance and it will do its job. Be sure to *hit down and through* the shot, catching the ball first and then the turf.

The short irons (8, 9 and pitching wedge) are control clubs. The swing should be shorter and more compact. The extreme loft of these clubs, plus the relatively short length of the shaft, make control much easier for the neophyte; hence, results can be achieved faster. Proper results with the short irons can best be achieved by keeping your swing under control and by making two adjustments in your stance. 1) Narrow your stance about five inches from the "shoulder width" position. 2) Use the *"open" stance.* The left foot is pulled back from the "square" line about two or three inches. This will "open" your whole body toward the target. The results with this change—plus the use of a shorter club—will be a shorter, more upright backswing, essential to control and accuracy. No conscious effort is needed to make this swing-change, as the swing is altered by the preliminary changes and by the length of the club.

LEARNING EXPERIENCE—ASSUMING AN OPEN STANCE
Set a club on the ground pointing at the target. Assume a normal stance. Now, narrow your stance about five inches. Pull the left foot away from the line two or three inches. Repeat this three or four times. Now, practice the short iron swing using this stance. The abbreviated backswing causes a more abrupt blow down into and through the ball, resulting in more backspin and control of the shot.

---

4. Consistent performance with the pitch shot will result in better scores for any player.

Now that you have the idea of the full swing and some of the shots out on the fairway, let's move in closer to the green, into "scoring country," and examine the shots that will get you close to the hole for a one-putt green. First, let's discuss the "pitch shot."

The expected result of the pitch shot will be a highly lofted shot with much backspin, so the ball will stop quickly when it lands on the green. It is most effective when you must hit over a hazard or obstacle, or when the flagstick is close to the near edge of the green. A 9-iron or pitching wedge would be the logical club selection for this shot. To execute this shot, do the following:

A) Your stance and grip remain the same as normal, with two exceptions: your feet should be fairly close together and adjusted to the open stance, and your hands should be lowered to the middle part of the grip for control. The ball is played in the same place—just inside the left heel.

B) Accentuate the balance of weight on the left leg and leave it there throughout the swing, using only a good shoulder turn in taking the club back.

C) Allow your hands to cock gradually in the backswing.

D) The length of your backswing will determine how far you hit the ball, and your follow-through will approximate the length of the backswing.

E) Take the club away in good control and accelerate the downswing briskly through the ball. It is easy to "baby" this shot. Hit down and through the ball with authority.

F) Keep the left hand firmly on the club throughout the swing.

Practice is the special key in learning how to use the pitch shot. Only through practice will you learn how to shorten or lengthen your backswing to adapt for different distances.

5. Success with the chip shot can be achieved very quickly by the beginner.

This shot is used when you are very close to the green. The distance between the edge of the green and the flagstick and the distance your ball is from the edge of the green will help, along with much practice, to determine which club to select for the shot. No matter what club is chosen, the idea is to get the ball on the green as quickly as possible and let it run to the cup. To execute this shot, do the following:

PITCH SHOT—Marilynn Smith (Courtesy of A. G. Spalding & Bros., Inc.;
Photographs by Harry Terry)

A) The stance for the chip shot is similar to the pitch shot stance, except that your feet are placed even closer together for control. The ball is still played off the inside of the left heel. The open stance enables you to envision your line to the cup and gets your left side out of the way, eliminating excessive body movement.

B) Your grip remains the same as always. The club is held near the lower end of the grip for better control.

C) The weight should be over the left foot at address, and should remain there throughout the shot.

D) The backswing is short and smooth. Many players use the "firm-wrist" method, while others cock their hands slightly in the backswing.

E) The downswing is also smooth and rhythmical: *down and through the ball.*

F) For extreme accuracy, the head and lower body must remain still throughout the swing. Allow the shoulders, arms and hands to execute the swing.

G) The clubhead should remain square to the intended line throughout the shot.

LEARNING EXPERIENCE—CHIPPING

Set up in your chipping posture and try a few swings, keeping your backswing very limited. Make sure that the clubhead does not pass ahead of the line of your left arm as you hit through the ball and to the finish. The back of your left hand should be facing the target. The clubface does not roll over, but is square to the intended line of flight.

---

6. Getting out of the sand is often a mental problem with the beginner, but with proper thought, good technique and practice this problem can be overcome.

Many experts feel that getting out of sand is quite simple and routine, whereas the beginner feels that this is the toughest problem in playing golf. The difference—knowledge gained through experience, technique and *practice, practice, practice!* Use the club and stroke that will get the most favorable results. Consider the following examples of common sense:

CHIP SHOT—Bruce Fleisher (Photographs by Harry Terry)

A) *Putt the ball.* If there is no overhanging lip on the edge of the bunker facing you and you have a nice level lie, the putter can be a most effective club. Practice with this shot will teach you just how hard to hit the ball to get it close to the cup. Generally the ball must be hit a great deal harder than when putting a ball on the green.

B) *Chip the ball.* If the bunker is shallow and the lie of the ball is level, try chipping the ball out with a normal chip shot, using a fairly lofted club such as an 8-iron or 9-iron. *Contact the ball first.* Usually you must hit this shot a bit harder than you would the same shot from a grassy lie.

C) *Explode the ball.* A normal explosion shot (cut shot or blast) from the sand is executed with a highly lofted club, preferably a sand wedge. The sole of the sand wedge is rounded so the club will not penetrate too deeply downward, but rather will slide through the sand. The stance and address closely resemble those used in the pitch shot. Open the face of the club slightly at address.

1) Remember that a bunker is a hazard and by the rules of golf you may not sole your club at address or touch the sand in the backswing.

EXPLOSION SHOT—Bruce Fleisher (Photographs by Harry Terry)

2) Work your feet down into the sand to establish a solid stance for good balance. This action will also help you determine the depth and texture of the sand. Since your feet are lower than the ball, it will be necessary to adjust your grip proportionately down on the club.

3) Concentrate your vision about one to two inches behind the ball. This is the point where the club should enter the sand. Experience will tell you how much sand to take.

4) The backswing is executed with little body turn but a good shoulder turn. Get the club up fast with a quicker wrist cock. This take-away and your open stance will create a "cutting" action on the downswing—outside to inside. With this swing, aim slightly to the *left* of the target.

5) Pull the club down and through the sand. The force of the sand exploding beneath the ball will get it out and on its way. Be sure to *follow-through completely*. Results will be a fairly high shot, little spin on the ball and a "soft" landing. Keep this shot firm like the pitch shot. Practice sound technique and it will soon become a conventional shot for you. Be sure to have a rake handy (rakes are found near each bunker), to smooth out the footprints made in the bunker.

One other shot out of the sand that demands a change in technique is the *buried lie*. This occurs when the ball lands directly in the sand and literally "buries" itself. A normal explosion shot usually will not remove the ball. Make the following changes:

1) Play the ball farther back in your stance and still use a slightly open stance. Select a club with a greater cutting edge, such as a pitching wedge or 9-iron.

2) Make sure that the face of the club is square to the intended line, or even slightly closed on a deep lie.

3) *Hit down on the ball hard!* Aim for the back edge of the ball. Do not be concerned with follow-through.

4) This is a survival shot; the ball will come out of the bunker with a low trajectory and have a lot of overspin on it. Be content to get the ball on the putting surface.

7. The putt is the most used and most important basic shot in the game of golf.

The putting game has been referred to as, "that other game," "cruel punishment that should not be a part of a gentleman's game" and a "different game." Whatever is said of this aspect of golf, it is the most vital part, and the putter is the most used club in the bag. During an 18-hole round, if you were to "2-putt" every green, you would use your putter a total of 36 times. For the expert player, this means using the putter for half his shots during a round of play, considering that an average par for 18 holes is 72. For the beginner, this average would rise considerably, but the putter would still be used a good 30 to 40 percent of the time. It's hard to fight the percentages; *to score well you must putt well.*

Actually, putting success is the easiest to achieve for the neophyte. A straight-faced club is used, the ball is rolled on the ground, the shot is relatively short and the style you use can be your own. There are as many putting styles as there are players. A few simple basics should be followed and, for the sake of consistency, practice is a must. Experience in playing the game will then help you develop your style.

A) *The Putting Grip.* Most any grip could be acceptable, however the most commonly used grip is the *reverse overlap.* The index finger of the left hand is placed over the little finger of the right hand. It can best be assumed by placing the right hand on the grip first. Some experts will overlap the little finger *and* the ring finger, or even overlap three fingers of the right hand. Experiment with this until you feel that the palms face each other. If the thumbs are placed on top of the grip, pointing down the shaft and in line with each other, chances are that your palms will be facing each other.

B) *The putting stance.* A comfortable stance is a prerequisite; maintain a good knee flex. Allow the arms to assume a bent position and keep them fairly close to the body. It is recommended that the right arm actually brush the right hip in the putting stroke. Bend from the waist far enough to get your eyes directly over the ball. The width of the stance is not important, except that it too should be comfortable. The ball position should be consistent. Try playing the ball directly opposite the left toe when you start and then, through practice, find the best placement for you. The weight should be concentrated over the left leg, although this too is a matter of comfort. Try different styles and find the one that works best for you.

C) *The putting stroke.* Keep these ideas in mind as you practice:

1) Keep your body perfectly steady. Let your arms, hands and shoulders do the moving. 2) Keep the putter as low to the ground as possible throughout the swing. 3) Keep the putter blade square to the intended line through the ball.

There are two accepted styles of putting strokes: the *arm-and-shoulder* method, in which the hands are inactive (the easiest and most consistent style for most beginners) and the *wrist* method, in which the wrists move to activate the club with a little support from the arms. Some good players use a combination of both; almost all players must combine both styles when they are faced with an extremely long putt. Experiment to see which style suits you the best.

Some players *stroke* the ball and let the putter head follow after the ball naturally. Others *tap* the ball and do not concern themselves with the follow-through. This is a very good style to use on short putts. Try the various methods and create your own style. No matter what style you decide on, strive for the three "C's"—COMFORT, CONSISTENCY AND CONFIDENCE.

CONCLUSION TO THE BASIC SKILLS

Golf, at its best, is a very demanding, difficult game where practice is a must if you wish to become successful. Yet, it is a most satisfying experience if you adhere to principle, play within your physical capabilities, use a bit of common sense and appreciate the beauty of a good shot and the grandeur of a golf course. The game will reach right out and grab you by the heart. Bad shots will make you want to practice harder; good shots will "bring you back"; but whatever the cause, you will want to play the game.

Now you're off-and-swinging, the beginning of a chapter in your life entitled "GOLF, THE GAME OF A LIFETIME."

Outcomes

After studying this concept, you should be able to:

1. State the three main factors that will determine your success in mastering the full golf swing, name the most important one and explain why it is so important.

2. Demonstrate a good ten-finger grip, listing and pointing out the checkpoints for both the left and right hands.

3. State the guidelines for determining the firmness of the grip.

4. Explain what is meant by the term "togetherness" of the hands in the grip.

5. Explain how the overlapping and interlocking grips differ from each other and the ten-finger grip, and the relative merits of each.

6. Demonstrate the overlapping grip. The interlocking grip.

7. List and describe the seven checkpoints of a good stance.

8. Explain and demonstrate the procedure for assuming a good square stance.

9. Explain what is meant by the statement "ball position is relative to the left heel."

10. List the steps in executing the backswing and the five points to check at the top of the backswing.

11. State what type of action in which parts of the body initiate and carry out the downswing.

12. Describe the position of the head during the downswing.

13. Explain what happens during the follow-through and why it isn't necessary to learn this part of the swing separately.

14. Execute the full swing properly.

15. Explain why the full swing is basic to the game and list those factors that may necessitate minor adjustments in your swing during play.

16. State the rule that gives you an advantage in hitting balls from the teeing ground.

17. Describe the principle to be followed by the beginner in hitting the tee shots.

18. Describe the principle to be followed in teeing-up the ball.

19. Hit a good tee shot with three different clubs.

20. Explain and demonstrate the two adjustments made in the basic swing when hitting a tee shot.

21. List the clubs generally used for full fairway shots.

22. Explain why no adjustment of the basic swing is needed when using fairway woods or long and medium irons.

23. Hit good full fairway shots using all possible clubs.

24. Describe the unique physical characteristics of the short irons and why these are good for beginners.

25. Describe the difference between a square and open stance and demonstrate each.

26. List and demonstrate the adjustments necessary in the basic swing when using a short iron.

27. Execute good shots with each short iron.

28. Describe the results of a good pitch shot.

29. Explain and demonstrate the procedures to be followed in executing a pitch shot.

30. Execute good pitch shots onto the green.

31. State the objective of a chip shot.

32. State and demonstrate the differences between the chip and pitch shot.

33. Execute good chip shots onto the green.

34. Explain why getting out of the sand poses a big problem for beginners, and how to overcome it.

35. Name three ways of getting out of the sand.

36. Describe the ways in which putting and chipping out of the sand differ from putting on the green and chipping on the fairway. Explain when each stroke should be used in the sand.

37. Describe and demonstrate the steps in hitting an explosion shot from the sand.

38. Explain and demonstrate the technique for hitting a buried lie.

39. Hit several sand shots using the putt, chip, explosion and buried lie explosion shot as is appropriate for the situation.

40. Explain why putting is considered the most important part of the game.

41. List three factors that make putting an easy skill for the neophyte to learn.

42. Describe and demonstrate the reverse overlap grip.

43. List the important principles governing the putting stance and stroke.

44. State the three "C's" of putting.

45. Execute a number of putts at various distances from the hole.

Concept IV—Foresight, Employed in Planning Each Shot from the Teeing Ground until the Ball Enters the Hole, Will Save Numerous Strokes and "Trouble Shots"

UP TO THIS point, most efforts have been directed toward the physical aspect of striking a golf ball and developing the various swings and shots necessary to score better. Let us now discuss the mental aspects of playing the game. After a proper warm-up and before approaching the first tee, the following principles should be foremost in mind:

1. Play within your physical limitations. Don't expect too much at first.
2. When in trouble (rough, bunkers and trees), get out with one shot.
3. When in doubt, hit the shot in which you have the most confidence.
4. Be observant of the conditions that prevail on the golf course (weather, grass, pin positions, etc.).
5. Once a shot-making decision is made, *concentrate* on striking the ball squarely.
6. Forget the bad shots in a hurry; you must face the test of the next shot immediately, so start thinking about how you will hit it.
7. Make every effort to keep the ball in play (on the fairway) at all times.

There are four basic areas of play involved in any golf hole: the teeing ground, the fairway, trouble (rough, bunkers, woods, bad lies, water, etc.) and the green. Let us begin at the tee and discuss some of the details involved in thinking one's way through the play of a golf hole.

ON THE TEE

A good tee shot will not only set up excellent scoring opportunities, but will also put the player in a good frame of mind. The ball should be kept on the fairway even if some distance must be sacrificed. It should be kept in mind that most shots curve in one direction or the other, so it is only intelligent golf to allow for that curve so that the ball will end up on the fairway. For example: if a golfer was slicing somewhat in the warm-up, he should aim his shot down the left side of the fairway and let it come back to the right. It makes good sense to tee the ball up on the side of the teeing ground where the trouble (woods, water, etc.) lies. By doing this a player almost automatically sets himself up to hit away from that trouble. A player should swing with good control when hitting the tee shot, particularly off the first tee. Swinging too hard usually leads to trouble.

Good position off the tee is the ultimate to the good player. To be able to hit the second shot from a level lie on the fairway and to have an open shot to the green is most desirable. Great players plan each shot on each hole, adjusting to weather factors, pin placements, tee marker placements and trouble shots.

A final word of advice for the tee shot and each shot that follows: make all mental decisions *before* assuming the address position, visualize the potential flight of the ball, then step up to the ball in a positive manner and execute the shot with little wasted time.

ON THE FAIRWAY

If the approach shot is a long one or the hole is a 5-par hole, chances are that a fairway wood (3-, 4- or 5-wood) would be the best club for the next shot. Club selection is based on many factors. A player should ask himself these questions:

1. What kind of lie does the ball have?
2. How will the wind affect the flight of the ball?
3. Is there moisture in the grass from rain or dew?
4. Where is the trouble around the green?
5. What is the exact placement of the flagstick?
6. Is the green elevated?
7. Will the green hold a properly hit iron shot? In other words, will the ball stop quickly or will it run a lot?
8. How far am I from the center of the green (in yards)? Every player should be observant of landmarks in the area where the

drive normally lands, especially if he plays that golf course enough to be able to *step off distances.* The reference points can be trees, bushes, poles, etc. The yardage stepped off from that point to the center of the green will give him approximate distances for his shots.

Once all of these factors have been assimilated by the player, and he has taken *his own shot-making ability* in mind, a club selection can be made with more confidence. Most average players frequently *fail to take a long enough club* for their shots.

When walking down the fairway a player should be observant of the pin placements on greens that he has yet to play. This will help him in positioning his tee shots and planning his approach shots for those holes. Finally, and most important, a good player will begin *concentrating* on the shot coming up just as soon as he can see the ball lying on the fairway or in the rough.

GETTING OUT OF TROUBLE

Remember the byword: *get out of trouble with one shot.* In many cases a player will take the "big gamble" and try to hit a shot that he is normally incapable of hitting. This will usually lead to more trouble. If a par or a birdie is needed in the competition, however, a calculated risk is one of the real thrills in golf. A player should carefully analyze his shot-making potential and consider the percentages involved in "pulling off" the shot. If the odds are not in his favor, it is only sound golf to get the ball out, on the fairway, and hopefully in a position in front of the green where there will still be a chance to salvage a par.

THE GREEN GAME

Thoughtful play around the green can save a player a lot of strokes, particularly the beginner. Emphasis has been placed on *practicing* these little shots: the crisp little pitch shot with a 9-iron, the firm chip shot and the controlled putt. Now the practice will pay off. Because only a part of a swing is involved, *the player should take a few practice swings until he gets the "feel" for that particular shot, then step up and execute it.*

Thoughts included in planning a *pitch shot* are much the same as for any approach shot. Because this shot is designed to stop quickly when it lands, it should be hit hard enough to get it near the flag on the fly. The tendency is to baby this shot, especially when it must be hit over a hazard. Be sure to hit *down and through* the shot, letting the club provide the loft. The contours of the green should be studied, particularly around the flagstick, and the player should form a mental picture of what the ball will do when it lands. The ball will slide and roll quite a bit going downhill and, conversely, will stop quickly going into an uphill pin position.

The key to good *chipping* is to *get the ball on the green and let it run to the cup.* Club selection for this shot is based on two factors: the distance the ball lies from the edge of the green and the distance the cup is from the edge of the green. If the pin is close to the edge, a more lofted club should be used; farther away, less loft. If the ball lies some distance from the green a more lofted club should be used; closer, less loft. Again, remember to study carefully the layout of the green, particularly around the cup. It is far better to leave a chip shot near the hole with an uphill putt remaining, rather than on the side or downhill angle. Concentrate, be firm in execution and believe in your club choice. The results achieved will be most gratifying.

LEARNING EXPERIENCE—THINKING FROM TEE TO GREEN
While practicing some day, try this game for a nice change in the routine. Visualize a given hole on the golf course. Tee the ball up and hit the tee shot. Depending on the length and direction the shot takes, try to imagine almost exactly where the ball now lies. Now concentrate on the second shot. Consider the factors involved, then execute the shot with proper club selection. If the game involves a third shot, use the same procedure until the ball is eventually on the imaginary green. Try this game using other holes on the golf course.

When *putting,* the contours of the green should be studied carefully, *especially* around the cup. The general line of the putt should be decided upon. Knowledge of the speed of the greens is necessary to know how hard to putt the ball. On long putts the idea of stopping the ball near the hole should be foremost in mind. *Distance is the big thought.* Practice swing—concentrate

—execute! On all short putts or any putt that is considered make-able, it is imperative to *get the ball up to the hole!* Short putts should generally be hit firmly to the back of the cup. On sidehill putts when the ball will curve considerably, especially as it nears the cup, the goal is to have the ball die (stop) in the cup. This type of putt can be dangerous if a player gets too bold. Three-putt greens can be averted with *proper thought before execution.* Every player should get comfortable over the ball and believe in his putting stroke.

Outcomes

1. List five generalities involved in planning one's play on the course.
2. Name the two key considerations in preparing to hit a tee shot.
3. Describe eight factors that must be considered when making a club selection.
4. Name the one thing that many beginners fail to do in selecting a club for an approach shot.
5. Repeat the byword for getting out of trouble.
6. List the key thought factors in hitting a short pitch shot.
7. Give the two factors that determine club selection for any chip shot.
8. State the philosophy of the short putt versus the long putt.

Concept V—You Must Develop the Ability to Hit a Variety of Shots, Such As Shots from Different Types of Lies and under Abnormal Weather Conditions, Shots with Different Lofts and Variances in Direction, and Shots That Intentionally Curve in One Direction or the Other to Move Beyond the State of the Novice

Now THAT YOU have the basic skills fairly well in mind and have had a chance to practice them, let us progress into some of the *different* shots that you will face when playing on the course. Confidence in these shots will develop only through practice and play.

1. Rough is trouble; get the ball out of it without wasting any shots.

Choose a club with enough loft to get the ball up and out; usually this will take a club with more loft than you would use from the same distance on the fairway. Play the ball in the middle of your stance. Pick out a target to the most open area entering into the green or even short of the green for good position. Get the club up quickly on the backswing (like the pitch shot). Hit down and *through* the ball with your normal tempo and let the club do the work. The ball will have overspin as it "flies" out of the deeper grass, due to the moisture in the grass that gets between the clubface and the ball, therefore it will roll quite a bit after landing. You might be surprised at how far (with roll) you can hit a ball out of rough grass with a more lofted club.

2. The ability to hit a ball high or low is a distinct advantage to any player.

Consider: a) playing in the wind, b) hitting an approach shot to a small elevated green, c) hitting over a clump of trees and

d) hitting under a large limb of a tree. Knowledge of the loft of your clubs and the angle of flight of the ball from that loft is most important. The following hints should help you in handling these shots:

The High Shot. In the address position, move your hands away from the target about three inches. Play the ball more toward the left foot. Use a slightly open stance. A slightly open clubface will also help to increase the loft of the shot, but be sure to consider your alignment if you do this. An open clubface will cause the ball to fly to the right of the intended line of flight.

The Low Shot. Be sure to have your hands ahead of the club head at address (left wrist covers the left knee). Play the ball more toward the right foot. Use a normal swing but follow-through lower. In either the high or low shot, unless you purposely want to open or close the clubface, be sure that the leading edge of the sole of the club is square to your intended line of flight.

LEARNING EXPERIENCE—HITTING SHOTS HIGH AND LOW
Make the minor adjustments as suggested and try to hit five consecutive shots over a convenient tree on the practice area. Use a 9-iron for this drill. Later, try the same thing with a 5-iron, moving away from the target somewhat due to the lesser loft of the 5-iron.

Now try to hit five consecutive shots that have a low trajectory. Again, try to hit under the branch of a tree that might be located in the practice area. Try this with two or three different clubs. Concentrate on technique, and try to recognize the height of each shot from each club.

---

3. If you wish to hit an extremely low shot with a lot of backspin on the ball, work on the "punch shot."

Set up as you would for the low shot, with your hands well ahead and the ball placed more toward the right foot. Do not activate the wrists much in your backswing. Concentrate on hitting *down* and low through the ball and don't be too concerned about following-through all the way. This is sometimes referred to as "blocking out" the hand action. The punch shot is most effective when playing into the wind or across the wind. It stays low and the added backspin helps the ball hold its intended line. Direction is the most important item to consider when playing in the wind. Only practice will help you determine the choice of clubs for various distances and the "use" of the wind to your advantage.

4. Many times you will be faced with shots that challenge you to curve the ball to the right (fade and slice) or to the left (draw shot and hook).

With their normal swing, most people curve the ball in one direction or the other. However, let's consider those situations that *demand* a curving shot, such as around a clump of trees or around a fairway with a dogleg.

Hitting from left to right (Fade and slice). For the fade, weaken the grip only *slightly* (rotate your hands on the grip counterclockwise). Take more club than you normally need, as you will lose yardage as the ball curves. Play the ball more toward the left heel. Open your stance slightly. Execute normally. The expected result will be a shot that flies fairly straight and then falls off to the right. To hit a slice, accentuate the changes just given. Open the clubface just slightly. Cock the wrists quickly outside the normal plane in the backswing, and then feel that you are hitting *away from* your intended target (outside-in swing). Alignment to the left is important—give yourself room to the left of the target.

Hitting from right to left (Draw shot and hook). To execute the draw shot, try the following changes: Strengthen your grip *slightly* (rotate your hands on the grip clockwise). Use a closed stance (drop your right foot back about three inches from the square line). Concentrate on keeping your head steady through impact. The expected result will be a fairly straight shot, with the ball curving slightly to the left near the end of its flight. To hook the ball (a sharp-breaking curve to the left), close the clubface just slightly. Accentuate the idea of hitting away from the target (an inside-out swing). Allowing the wrists to roll over immediately after impact will increase the amount of hook. Allow room to the right in your alignment for the resulting curve to the left.

LEARNING EXPERIENCE—CURVING THE BALL TO THE
LEFT AND RIGHT
Review the changes in technique for hitting the cut shot. Now, try to
hit five consecutive shots that have good carry and curve slightly off
to the right. Do the same thing with the slice. Execute five in a row.
Notice the alignment changes that you must make. Try a 5-iron with
these shots.

Follow the same procedure with the draw shot and the hook shot.
Again, be aware of lining-up correctly and always hit toward a defi-
nite target.

---

5. Uneven lies present an interesting challenge to all golfers.

Here are the four typical situations and some simple rules to
follow in executing the shot involved:

A) *Uphill.* Position the ball toward the higher (left) foot. Brace
yourself well inside your right leg, while trying to keep the balance of weight on the left leg. The biggest problem in executing
this shot is swaying your weight to the right in the backswing.
Align yourself to hit slightly to the right of the target, because
the ball will tend to be pulled or even hooked to the left. (Only
experience will tell you how much to allow for varying degrees
of slopes.) Use a club with less loft, for the ball will fly higher
and will not have as much carry as from a level lie. Remember,
on any uneven lie, *balance* is the real key to success. To help
achieve this, bend the knees a bit more than usual and use a
shorter swing.

B) *Downhill.* Position the ball more toward the higher (right)
foot. Practice swings will help you determine this position.
Watch where the clubhead hits the grass. Brace yourself well
on the left leg, as the tendency in this shot is to sway off the
ball to the left during the downswing. Use an open stance, as
this will allow your backswing to be more upright and provide
greater comfort and balance. Aim to the left of your intended
line, as this shot will have a tendency to be pushed or even
sliced to the right. Select a more highly lofted club than normal,
as the downslope causes the ball to fly low.

C) *Sidehill—Ball Above Feet.* Play the ball more toward the middle of your stance and open your stance slightly. Keep your

weight forward on the balls of your feet for balance. Your hands should be placed farther down the grip to adjust to the closeness of the ball. Because your swing will take on a much flatter plane due to the contour of the hill, you will have a tendency to pull or even hook this shot, therefore make your point of aim to the right of your intended line, and use a club with less loft than you would use from a level lie to compensate for the loss of distance involved when the ball curves a lot. *Remember, don't force these shots! Use a shorter swing!*

D) *Sidehill—Ball Below Feet.* Grip the club as long (near the butt end) as you can and play the ball toward the middle of your stance. Keep your weight back on the heels and get a good flex in the knees to compensate for the distance between your hands and the clubhead. Your swing will now be more upright, therefore the ball will tend to be pushed or sliced to the right of your target. Align yourself more to the left to allow for this. Use a club with less loft to compensate for the curve pattern of the ball.

Experience and practice will dictate the correct solution to shot problems. If you incorporate all your knowledge on clubs, grips, stances, ball positions, types of grasses, terrain and potential shot results, you should come up with a satisfactory solution to any shot you may have to face. A sound swing, practice and more practice, and experience in playing the game will minimize the number of these types of shots that you will have to face. However, no matter how long you play the game, these shots will confront you along with many others that you will have to solve in order to score better. You are on your own! Each shot is a new challenge! *This is the thrill in golf!*

Outcomes

Your success in moving beyond the state of a novice in golf will be dependent on doing certain things. Do the following:

1. Describe the changes from normal you must make in preparing to hit a ball out of the rough.
2. Give the reason for a "flyer" out of the rough.

3. List three adjustments you must make in your set up to hit a high ball.

4. Describe the swing changes that must be made for the punch shot.

5. Give the adjustments necessary in making a ball slice.

6. Demonstrate a closed stance.

7. Describe the feeling you must have when hooking the ball.

8. List the differences between hitting a shot from an uphill lie and from a downhill lie.

9. Describe the setup and hitting philosophy of the sidehill, ball-above-feet shot as contrasted to the sidehill, ball-below-feet shot.

10. List the conditions that will affect your decision in club selection.

11. Try hitting a few shots with the cut shot swing changes. Now try to slice a few shots with the same club.

12. Execute the punch shot with a short iron.

13. Practice drawing the ball with a 5-iron. Now try a few shots with the intention of hooking them.

Concept VI—Rules Pertaining to the Game of Golf May Be Categorized under One of Six Major Headings: 1) Rule of Etiquette; 2) No Penalty; 3) One-Stroke Penalty; 4) Stroke-and-Distance Penalty; 5) General Penalty; 6) Disqualification Penalty

THE OFFICIAL RULES of golf in the United States are those approved by the United States Golf Association and The Royal and Ancient Golf Club of St. Andrews, Scotland. Each year the USGA publishes an inexpensive rule book. Certain local rules authorized by the USGA are included to cover the physical characteristics of individual golf courses. These local rules, if employed, should appear on the scorecard and be posted at the first tee. Even the novice should play the game by employing only the official rules and the local rules authorized by the USGA. If he disregards any of these rules, he should not call the game he is playing *golf!*

1. There are two distinct types of competition, match play and stroke play.

Some rules differ regarding the penalty awarded for a breach in each type of play.

1a. Match play is based on the number of holes won, the winner of each hole being determined by low score on the hole. Each player competes against an opponent. When a handicap stroke is awarded on a hole, the lower net (score less handicap stroke) *on each hole* wins the hole. A match, consisting of a stipulated round (18 holes, unless altered by the committee), is won when one player is ahead by more holes than the number of holes remaining in the match. In case of a tie at the end of the round, the players tee-off on the first hole and proceed until one player wins a hole. If it becomes necessary to have a decision made in match play, or if there is any doubt as to how a player should proceed, he must get a ruling before he plays from the next tee. If a dispute occurs on the last hole of the round, the decision must be made before the players leave the putting green. No claim can be made by a player later if this procedure is not followed, unless his opponent gave him wrong information.

1b. The winner in stroke play is the person with the lowest score at the end of a number of stipulated rounds. If the tournament is a handicap event, the player with the lowest net score wins. When players tie, they must play another 18-hole round to determine the winner (unless altered by the committee). In stroke play a claim can be made at any time before the results of the tournament are officially announced. If a player is not certain as to how he should proceed at any time during the round, he may play out the hole with the ball he is playing. In addition, he may also play the hole with a second ball from the point of doubt, announcing his intention to play the ball under this rule and indicating which ball he wants to score if the rules permit. Upon completing the round he must immediately get a ruling from the committee.

Every golfer, regardless of whether he intends to play golf competitively or socially, should study the rules of golf carefully and should carry an official rulebook in his golf bag. The book is well indexed, and even the novice will be able to find the decision governing a particular situation. Although he will find the rules specific, he will often find them difficult to interpret.

It is hoped that the organization of most of the rules by the penalty involved will enable you to learn and retain the related concepts. The rules of etiquette and the rules of the game which govern situations for which relief is granted without penalty are easy to remember, once they are brought to your attention. The infringements of the rules for which penalties are incurred are those most difficult to retain. After studying the first two concepts (rule of etiquette; no penalty) and learning the penalties for the breaches of rules in the concepts dealing with one-stroke penalty, stroke-and-distance penalty, and disqualification, you will become aware that most violations of the rules for which penalties are awarded are included under the general penalty, including *most* of the breaches not discussed in this text. This discussion is not a substitute for the official rulebook. Rather, it is the authors' intent to help you understand the rules governing the most frequently occurring situations.

2. The courtesies of play or golf etiquette, although not classified as official rules in the strict sense, are important for enjoyable play.

The use of proper etiquette when playing golf is as important as the display of proper manners in any other situation. Observance of the rules of etiquette does not complicate play, but rather heightens the enjoyment of the game for everyone. As a result, players will be permitted to concentrate and perform without distractions, play will be faster and golf courses will stay in better playing condition. The courtesies of play may be classified under where they apply on the course: 1) general; 2) teeing ground; 3) through the green; 4) bunker; 5) putting green.

2a. General rules of etiquette apply anywhere on the course.

1) Proper attire for a woman consists of a blouse worn with either a skirt, culotte, bermuda-length short or slack. Ideally, golf shoes should be worn. Men should wear a shirt with either a slack or bermuda-length short.
2) Every player should have a bag with at least the minimum equipment necessary to play the game.
3) All local rules should be read before teeing-off, and followed when on the course.
4) Talking excessively while playing a hole may prevent others from concentrating on their shots.
5) Golfers must learn to control their tempers when playing on a course. There is no excuse for profanity or loudness.
6) Do not move ahead of the ball farthest from the hole. Besides being a discourtesy, it is an extremely dangerous practice. Balls are sometimes hit sharply to the right or left of a player.
7) In order to play without delay, the shot to be made should be planned as one walks to the ball. Care should be taken not to take too many practice swings (warm-up swings before an attempt is made to stroke the ball).
8) Do not hit your ball until the group ahead is out of the range

of your best shot. If there is any danger that the ball may hit someone, call "FORE" loudly.

9) Learn to mark your ball near some stationary object. Try also to "spot" the balls of the other members of your group.

10) Whether the balls are on or off the green, the ball farthest from the hole should be played first.

11) Teaching on the course should be done only by the club professional. The place to help a friend is on the practice range.

12) Practice strokes should not be taken unless the course is empty and your intent is to practice for a tournament. A practice swing without attempting to hit a ball is not a practice stroke.

13) When you must take a penalty stroke, announce this to your group at once.

14) If you are playing slowly and there is more than one clear hole ahead of your group, signal those immediately behind to play through. Be certain that all take cover off the fairway, if it is not feasible to wait until the next tee is reached before allowing them to pass your group.

15) If you are given permission to play through another group, be certain to thank them for this courtesy.

2b. Some rules of etiquette are related specifically to the teeing ground.

1) Carts and bags should be placed off the teeing ground to the side of the markers nearest where the group is to wait.

2) The person who has the "honor" (entitled to play first), whether through draw or lot, should be allowed to tee-off first on the first hole. Low score determines the honor on successive holes. The honor is retained until someone scores better on a hole.

3) When awaiting your turn to hit, stand facing the person teeing-off at a reasonable distance off the teeing ground.

4) Do not talk or move as a player is preparing to stroke the ball. Either act may break his concentration.

5) Before teeing-off, be certain that your ball has identifying marks different from that of any other player in your group. It is courteous to offer to change your ball when necessary for identification purposes.

6) Do not distract others in your group by teeing your ball before it is your turn to hit.

7) A provisional ball (a ball played only for a ball which may be lost or out-of-bounds) should be played after everyone else has hit his first tee shot. If more than one person must hit a provisional ball, play should be in the same order established before hitting the first ball.

2c. Certain courtesies should be adhered to when playing "through the green," the area of the course exclusive of the teeing ground, hazards and putting green.

1) While searching for a ball which cannot be readily found, wave the group behind to pass. Be certain to take cover behind a tree or your cart! Everyone in your group should then aid in the search. Take your place on the course, after looking for the five minutes allowed, but do not hit until the group ahead is well out of your range.
2) Turf taken when hitting a shot should be replaced, pressing it down.
3) Allow the player who is hitting from his own fairway the right-of-way. Players who hit on adjacent fairways must wait their turn.
4) Do not hit to a green until the group ahead is well on its way to the next tee. No matter how accurate you think you may be, there is always danger of hitting someone.
5) Upon nearing the green, care should be taken to keep one's cart and bag off the slopes of the green. Place them to the side or behind the green nearest the next tee.

2d. Several rules of etiquette are frequently violated when a player's ball lands in a bunker.

1) Place the bags well away from the fringe of the hazard.
2) Never enter a bunker except to play a ball.
3) If two balls lie in a bunker, the player whose ball lies farthest from the hole should be allowed to enter the hazard first. When he is finished the second player should be given the same privilege.
4) Enter and leave the bunker at a point near the ball, thus making the fewest footprints possible. If the bunker has a high lip, enter it from the lower edge.
5) Be sure to rake the trap well upon leaving it.

2e. There are numerous rules of etiquette to be followed when on the putting green.

1) Repair all ball marks immediately, using a tee or similar article to level the turf and fill in the ball mark. Lift the depressed area with the tee, then smooth the mark with the weight of your putter.
2) If a caddie is not present, the one whose ball lies closest to the hole should attend the flagstick when another player wishes to have it attended.
3) When the flagstick is no longer needed by anyone in the group, it should be placed well out of the way. Be careful not to drop it!
4) Stand well out of the putter's view as he is lining up and stroking his putt.
5) Be certain that your shadow covers neither the hole nor the line of another's putt.
6) Learn to mark your ball correctly. If a fellow player feels your ball may interfere with his success in making his next shot, he may ask you to mark your ball. If this request is made, place a coin behind the outermost point of the ball before picking it up. If it is in the line of another's putt, mark it one or two putterheads to the side, moving the coin or marker to this point. Replace the ball in the same manner before picking up the marker.
7) Do not step anywhere on the line from someone's ball to the hole. The indentations made by your footprints may cause others to miss their putts.
8) Do not drag your feet. Besides ruining the green, a player's putt may be thrown aside by the raised grass.
9) Caution should be taken not to step near the hole at any time. Putts which otherwise might have been holed out will often hang on the edge when the area around the cup is injured.
10) Upon holing out (hitting the ball in the cup), remove the ball from the cup at once. A ball, allowed to remain, may keep another player's ball from staying in the cup.
11) The player who holes out first, in the absence of a caddie, should take the responsibility for replacing the flagstick. The last one to putt should not be left to replace it.
12) Do not leave the green, except to stand on the fringe, until all have finished putting. It is discourteous to start toward

the next tee before all have holed out. Move quickly off the green toward the next tee when all in your group have finished, so the group behind will not need to wait any longer than necessary to play their shots to the green.

13) Settle all points of dispute and mark the scores only after moving a safe distance from the green to the next tee.

3. Certain conditions not under the control of the golfer create a situation which warrants relief without penalty.

Relief from natural hazards such as water and bunkers, trees and bushes requires that a person incur a penalty in order to be allowed relief from the situation. A local rule may offer relief without penalty, however, to protect a young tree or shrub (marked by stakes) while it is growing. Listed below are some of the other conditions under which a player may obtain relief from a situation without incurring a penalty:

NO PENALTY

1. Ball falling off tee while player is addressing it.
2. Movable obstructions (artificial).
3. Immovable obstructions (artificial).
4. Playing out of turn.
5. Hole made by an animal, ground under repair and casual water.
6. Dropped ball, resting against you, moves.
7. Dropped ball rolling into a hazard, out-of-bounds, more than two club-lengths or nearer the hole (re-drop).
8. Ball on wrong green.
9. Opponent's ball moved by your ball in match play.
10. Opponent's ball (at rest) moved by you, your caddy, ball or equipment in stroke play.
11. Ball moving on green when loose impediments are removed.
12. Ball being moved on fairway within designated distance (no closer) to the hole, when playing "winter rules."
13. Teeing-off outside the teeing ground in match play.

An interpretation regarding the relief awarded in each of these cases is listed below:

1) No penalty is incurred if the ball falls or is knocked off the

tee as you address it, provided you made no attempt to hit it. You may re-tee your ball.

2) Any movable obstruction such as a hose, bench, rake, directional flag or stake defining a water hazard may be removed. No penalty is incurred if the ball is moved in the process, but it must be replaced on the exact spot from which it was moved. Fences and stakes defining out-of-bounds are not considered obstructions and may not be removed.

3) If a ball lies on or touches an immovable obstruction such as a shed, bridge or bridge supports, not part of the bank in the confines of a water hazard, or is within two club-lengths of an immovable obstruction which interferes with one's stance, backswing or stroke to be taken in the direction of the hole, relief may be taken without a penalty. If on the putting green, you may place the ball within two club-lengths of the outside of the obstruction nearest the point where the ball was lying originally; if through the green or in a hazard, you may drop the ball at a similar point no nearer the hole. You may not measure under or through the obstruction. For rules governing a proper drop, see #6 under one-stroke penalty.

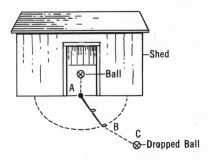

Upon dropping the ball in the above case, the ball could roll two more club lengths legally, for a total of four club lengths.

4) A stroke, played out of turn in stroke play, stands. In match play, if you choose, you may let it stand or you may immediately require your opponent to replay the stroke. If required to replay the shot, he does not incur a penalty. He disregards the ball played out of turn and plays in the correct order.

5) If a ball touches or lies in a hole, an area marked as ground under repair by the committee (such as material piled up for removal and bare patches) or casual water (any temporary collection of water visible when the player takes his stance,

not meant to be a hazard or water hazard), relief may be obtained without incurring a penalty. If through the green, a ball may be dropped as near as possible to the spot where it lies, but not nearer to the hole, on the ground where conditions are favorable. In a hazard, the ball must be dropped in the hazard. If no relief is available in the hazard, a penalty stroke is incurred if the drop is then taken outside the hazard, keeping the point where the ball lay between the player and the hole. On the putting green the ball may be *placed* in the nearest position affording relief, but not nearer the hole. Even if a ball is lost under these conditions (some evidence necessary), no penalty is awarded. The ball should be dropped nearest the point where it last crossed the margin of the area on ground affording relief, but no closer to the hole.

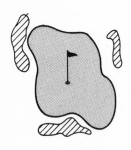
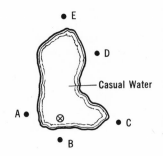

LEARNING EXPERIENCE—PROPER SPOT TO DROP FOR
CASUAL WATER
Each point a–e affords the minimum distance one can stand and ground his club without being in the casual water. Select the letter or letters where it would be legal to drop. (Answer at the end of the concept.)

---

6) If a dropped ball comes to rest against you and moves when you do, you receive no penalty. The ball is played as it lies.
7) If a ball, properly dropped, rolls nearer the hole, into a hazard, out-of-bounds or more than two club-lengths, it may be re-dropped without penalty. If it must be placed, because of irregularities preventing a drop of this type, it may be placed nearest where it was last dropped, but no nearer the hole.

8) There is no penalty given for removing a ball lying on the putting green of a hole not being played at that time. It should be lifted and dropped away from the green as nearly as possible to where the ball lay, but no closer to the hole. If it rolls nearer the hole or into a hazard it may be re-dropped without penalty.

9) No matter how close either ball lies to the cup, there is no penalty if one's ball moves an opponent's ball when one is engaged in match play. The opponent may play his ball as it lies or, before another stroke is taken by either side, may replace his ball on the spot from which it was moved. If he were lying four on the green, after which his ball was holed out for him by his opponent's ball, his score for the hole would be four.

10) No penalty is incurred if you move your opponent's ball, which is at rest, when you are playing stroke play. He must replace his ball before playing another stroke. (*Exception:* on putting green.)

11) Loose impediments such as rocks and leaves lying on the putting green may be picked up or brushed aside with one's hand or club, provided nothing is pressed down in the process. If the ball moves, it may be replaced without penalty.

12) Although "preferred lies" or "winter rules" are not endorsed by the USGA, they are often observed under local rules when the fairways are in poor condition. If employed, the lie of the ball may be improved within a designated distance (usually six inches) no closer to the hole, only when you are on your own fairway (the fairway of the hole being played). If a ball is moved after it is placed, a stroke must be counted.

13) In match play, if a player tees his ball outside the teeing ground (area within two club lengths behind the outside point of the markers and bordered by the side of the markers), his opponent may have him replay the stroke from within the teeing ground. A penalty is awarded only in stroke play.

4. The least serious penalty awarded for a breach of a rule is a one-stroke penalty.

For infringements of the rules and relief from the situations included under this concept, a one-stroke penalty is awarded. The situations under this section pertaining to water hazards and un-playable lies is one option that may be taken; the other option will be found under the stroke-and-distance penalty.

ONE-STROKE PENALTY

1. Moving one's ball accidentally after addressing it, except on the tee.
2. You, your partner or either of your caddies accidentally moving your ball which is at rest.
3. You, your caddie or equipment moving your opponent's ball (at rest) in match play (exceptions).
4. Moving the ball "through the green" when removing loose impediments.
5. Hitting the ball twice when making a forward swing.
6. Improper dropping.
7. Dropping behind a hazard when ball touches or lies in casual water, ground under repair or hole in the hazard.
8. Failing to continuously putt when on the green when playing stroke play (exceptions).
9. Cleaning the ball after the player has made a stroke on the putting green (except when playing local rule).
10. Obtaining relief from unplayable lies (two options).
11. Obtaining relief from water hazards:
    a. direct water hazard (one option under this concept).
    b. lateral water hazard (three options under this concept).

An explanation of each situation listed under "One-Stroke Penalty" is given below:

1) Except when teeing-off, if your ball moves accidentally after you have addressed it (taken your stance prior to making a stroke, having also grounded your club, except when in a hazard—when only the stance is taken), you incur a one-stroke penalty.
2) A penalty stroke is incurred if you, your partner or either of your caddies accidentally move your ball which is at rest. The ball is played as it lies.
3) It is also a one-stroke penalty if either you, your caddie or equipment touches or moves an opponent's ball which is at rest when playing match play. The exception of moving your opponent's ball accidentally while searching for it is not a penalty. The ball must be replaced before another stroke is made.

4) Through the green, if you, your partner or either of your caddies touch a loose impediment lying within a club's length of your ball, causing it to move (leave its position and come to rest in another place), you incur a one-stroke penalty. The ball is then played as it lies.

5) If you should strike the ball twice while executing a single stroke, you must add a one-stroke penalty besides counting the stroke attempted.

6) When a ball is to be dropped according to the rules, it must be dropped by *you* (the player). You must face the hole, stand up straight and drop the ball behind you over your shoulder. If the ball is dropped incorrectly and is not corrected before the next stroke is taken, a penalty stroke is incurred.

7) If you wish relief from a hazard when your ball lies in, touches or is lost (evidence to treat as *lost* requires that members in your group saw the ball go into the hazard) in casual water, ground under repair or a hole made by an animal, reptile or bird, you may take a one-stroke penalty and drop out of the hazard. In so doing, you must drop behind the hazard, no nearer the hole and as near as possible to the spot where the ball was, keeping the hazard and that point between you and the hole.

8) In stroke play, once you start putting on the putting green, you must continue to putt until you hole out. An exception is made when the opponent wishes one to mark his ball instead of putting, so that he will not step in the line of his putt.

9) When the ball lies on the putting green, it may be cleaned only before the player plays his first stroke (exception: local rule).

10) You may declare your ball unplayable anywhere on the course except in a water hazard, and you are the sole judge regarding this decision. Under a penalty of one stroke you may either a) drop it within two club-lengths of the spot where it laid, no closer to the hole, or b) keeping the spot where the ball lay between you and the hole, drop the ball on an extension of this line as far behind (away from the hole) as you wish. If the ball lies in a bunker other than in casual water, ground under repair or a hole made by an animal, the ball must be dropped in the bunker. Relief under these exceptions was listed under one-stroke penalty (7).

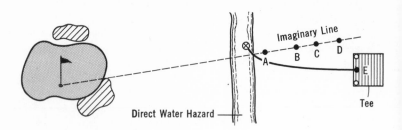

11a) To obtain relief from a ball lying in a water hazard (the ball is considered in the hazard if it lies inside the margin, even if it is out of the water itself), you may draw an imaginary line between where the ball last crossed the margin of the water hazard and the hole. You may drop the ball on an extension of this line as far behind the hazard as you wish (see figure, points a–d), being sure to keep the hazard between yourself and the hole.

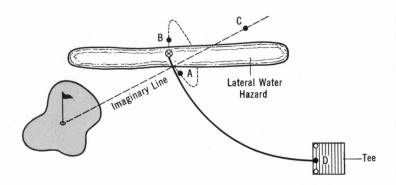

11b) A lateral water hazard is a water hazard which runs approximately parallel to the line of play. Relief may be taken with a one-stroke penalty in any of the following ways: 1) by dropping the ball within two club-lengths opposite the point where it last crossed the margin of the water hazard *on either side* of the lateral water hazard (figure, points a and b). The dropped ball must not land nearer the hole; 2) by drawing an imaginary line between the point where the ball last crossed the margin of the water and the hole, dropping the ball on an extension of this line as far behind the hazard as you wish, keeping the hazard between yourself and the hole (figure, point c).

5. There are only four breaches of the rules for which one may incur a stroke-and-distance penalty.

When this penalty is mandatory or when it is selected as an option, such as in the case of a water hazard or unplayable lie, you must count the stroke made, add a penalty stroke and lose the entire distance the ball traveled. If you hit your ball from the tee and elect to re-tee it for any of four reasons listed below, you will be shooting three from the tee.

STROKE-AND-DISTANCE PENALTY

1. Water hazards:
   a) direct water hazard (one option).
   b) lateral water hazard (one option).
2. Unplayable lie (one option).
3. Ball "out-of-bounds."
4. Lost ball.

An interpretation for each stroke-and-distance penalty is listed below:

1a and b) A stroke-and-distance penalty may be selected as an option for a direct water hazard or a lateral water hazard. In either case, this would mean taking the next shot from the tee or the approximate place of the last shot. (Refer to figures on page 66.)

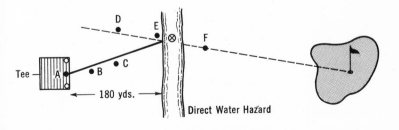

LEARNING EXPERIENCE—DIRECT WATER HAZARD

Only two of the six options described below are points from which a ball entering a water hazard from the tee may be played: a) from teeing ground; b) 45 yds. in front of the tee in line of entry; c) 90 yds. in front of the tee in line of entry; d) 75 yds. behind water on line from entry to hole; e) five ft. from point of entry (margin); f) two club-lengths from point of entry in line to hole. Which are the two alternatives? (Answer (2) at end of concept.)

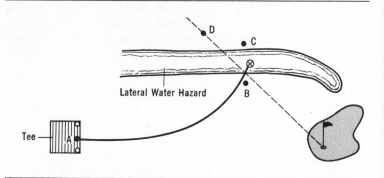

Lateral Water Hazard

Tee

LEARNING EXPERIENCE—LATERAL WATER HAZARD

Four options are given below as possible points from which to play a ball entering a lateral water hazard: a) teeing ground; b) within five ft. of the margin of the water where the ball entered; c) within three ft. of the margin of the water on the other side of the hazard opposite where the ball entered; d) 30 ft. in the adjacent fairway, on a line drawn between the point where the ball crossed the margin of the water and the hole. How many are legal options? (Answer (3) at end of concept.)

2) The third option for an unplayable lie (see 10 under one-stroke penalty for two other options) may be taken under the stroke-and-distance option. If you have played the stroke from the tee, you count that stroke, lose the distance and return to any point on the teeing ground and re-tee, adding one penalty stroke. You will now be "lying two" or "shooting three." If through the green, you must drop the ball as close as possible to the original spot from where the ball was hit. If in a hazard, the ball must be dropped in the hazard. If on the putting green, it may be placed.

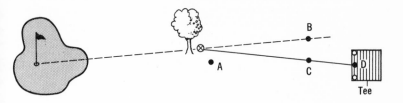

LEARNING EXPERIENCE—UNPLAYABLE LIE

One of these four options is illegal: a) two club-lengths from the ball; b) point on extension of line from ball to cup ten yds. away; c) anywhere on line from tee to ball; d) spot from which original ball was hit. Decide which one is incorrect. (Answer (4) at end of concept.)

---

3 and 4) If there is any doubt as to whether a ball is out-of-bounds or lost outside a water hazard, a provisional ball may be hit from as nearly as possible to the spot where the original ball was played. On the tee it may be re-teed, through the green it must be dropped, and on the putting green, placed. This ball will then be considered the ball in play unless the original ball is found and is in-bounds. Upon announcing your intention to hit the provisional ball, you do not need to give your reason for hitting it, but you should hit the provisional ball before you go to look for the original ball. You may stroke the provisional ball as many times as necessary until you reach the spot where the original ball is likely to be. A ball is declared lost if it cannot be found within five minutes from the time the search begins, or when you declare it lost. A ball is declared out-of-bounds when all of it lies outside the line drawn between the inside boundaries of the stakes or fenceposts. If a line is used to define out-of-bounds, the line itself is out-of-bounds. If any part of the ball is visible inside the boundaries (even if only a minute part), it is considered in-bounds. If the ball is lost or out-of-bounds, you count that stroke, lose the distance and add a penalty stroke. If it was your first stroke that went out-of-

bounds or was lost from the tee, the provisional ball hit from the tee to the fairway becomes your third stroke. You will now be "lying three" and "shooting four" from the fairway.

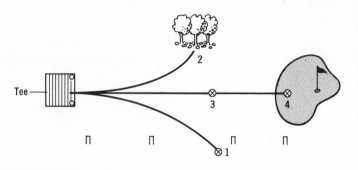

LEARNING EXPERIENCE—OUT-OF-BOUNDS AND LOST BALL
The first ball hit by you goes out-of-bounds. 1). The second ball hit from the tee lands in a pile of leaves and cannot be found; 2). The third ball hit as a provisional ball lands in the fairway; 3). After declaring the second ball lost, you hit the provisional ball to the green. What do you lie on the green? (Answer (5) at end of concept.)

---

6. Unless a penalty for a breach of a rule is provided for, it will usually fall under the heading "general penalty."

When in doubt as to the penalty for a breach of a rule, it is safe to assume that it fits under the general penalty. When a general penalty applies to a violation and you are playing a match, you lose the hole; in stroke play you incur a two-stroke penalty. Since this list of general violations is virtually endless, no attempt will be made to include every situation for which this penalty is awarded. Some of the most frequently occurring breaches are listed below:

General Penalty	Match Play	Stroke Play
1. Hitting wrong ball (exception: hazard)	Loss of hole	Two-stroke penalty
2. Grounding club in a hazard	Loss of hole	Two-stroke penalty

General Penalty	*Match Play*	*Stroke Play*
3. Removing loose impediment from hazard when ball lies in it	Loss of hole	Two-stroke penalty
4. Playing ball under wrong rule (rule which does not govern the case)	Loss of hole	Two-stroke penalty
5. Hitting the unattended flagstick when the ball lies on the green	Loss of hole	Two-stroke penalty
6. Striking the opponent's ball with your ball when both balls are on the green	No penalty	Two-stroke penalty
7. Using more than 14 clubs	Loss of a hole at each hole where infringement occurred; loss of two holes (max.) per round Penalty applied to the state of the match at the hole where the violation was discovered	Two strokes per hole for violation at that hole; four strokes max. per round
8. Pushing or scraping ball instead of clearly tapping it	Loss of hole	Two-stroke penalty
9. Giving or asking for advice which will aid one in playing the hole (information may be given regarding a rule)	Loss of hole	Two-stroke penalty

General Penalty	Match Play	Stroke Play
10. Improving one's lie or stance by bending or breaking something growing, except in legally taking one's stance	Loss of hole	Two-stroke penalty
11. Cleaning ball lying through the green (exceptions)	Loss of hole	Two-stroke penalty
12. Playing a ball which started to move before he began his backward stroke	Loss of hole	Two-stroke penalty
13. Dropping a ball and playing it from a point other than where it may be legally dropped	Loss of hole	Two-stroke penalty
14. Playing practice strokes (*not swings*) during the play of a hole	Loss of hole	Two-stroke penalty
15. Pressing down scuff marks made by golf shoes when they are in the line of one's putt	Loss of hole	Two-stroke penalty
16. a) Your ball in motion is deflected by you, your partner or either of your caddies or equipment.	Loss of hole	Two-stroke penalty

General Penalty	Match Play	Stroke Play
b) Your ball in motion is accidentally deflected by an opponent, his caddie or equipment (exception: when he is attending the flagstick)	Opponent loses hole	No penalty for rub of green (deflected by outside agency); play ball as it lies

The situations listed under this heading are so numerous that only three of the most frequently occurring situations will be discussed. The remaining decisions, if not self-explanatory, may be clarified by consulting the official rulebook or *Golf Rules In Pictures,* a publication of the USGA.

1) You must hole out with the ball hit from the tee, unless you are permitted by rule to substitute another ball, such as for a ball cut in play. An exception to this rule exists in both match and stroke play when a wrong ball is hit from a hazard. In such a case, there is no penalty if you then play your own ball from its original lie. The strokes played with a ball other than your own do not count, and the ball hit by mistake is replaced as nearly as possible to its original lie. In match play, whoever hits the wrong ball first loses the hole. If this cannot be determined, the hole should be played out with the balls exchanged. In stroke play, each player who plays a wrong ball incurs a two-stroke penalty. Each must return to the spot where his ball was and play it, ignoring all strokes played with the wrong ball. If the mistake is not rectified before the players tee-off on the next hole or leave the green, if it occurs on the last hole of the round, they will be disqualified.

2 and 3) You may not touch the ground or water in a hazard before making a stroke when your ball lies in or touches it. Neither may you touch or move a loose impediment lying in or touching a hazard, nor test (take a practice swing) any similar hazard. There is no penalty if your club touches grass or any other growing substance, or a stone wall, provided the club is not soled. If your ball is covered by sand, a pile of

leaves or similar items, you may remove enough so as to see the top of the ball. No penalty is awarded if the ball is moved, but it must be replaced. Your ball may not be identified by lifting it. If another ball in the sand interferes with your stroke, you may have it lifted and then replaced. If either ball is moved, no penalty is incurred and the ball may be replaced.

7. The most serious of all penalties is disqualification.

When you fail to abide by the original decision which governs the case, the committee may disqualify you from the competition. There are also other infractions of the rules whereby you may be disqualified.

DISQUALIFICATION PENALTY

1. Refusing to comply with any rule. Example: continuing to use more than 14 clubs upon discovery of extra clubs.
2. Deciding to waive any rule or penalty incurred.
3. Practicing on the competition course on the day of a round (stroke play) or between rounds when the tournament is scheduled on consecutive days.
4. Failing to count each stroke hit from outside the markers and to re-tee from the proper area (stroke play).
5. Failing to rectify a mistake before teeing-off on the next hole when a wrong ball has been played on the hole before (stroke play).
6. Repeated offense for undue delay.
7. Failing to start at the time scheduled and in the order set by the committee.
8. Failing to check the scorecard and co-sign it with the marker.

The above list includes those most common breaches of the rules for which the disqualification penalty is given. They are self-explanatory!

Review the five charts and attempt to digest the rules according to the penalty incurred. Only when you play by the rules of the game are you playing *golf!*

Outcomes

Answers to Learning Experiences
1. b; 2. a, d; 3. a, c, d; 4. c; 5. 6

After studying the courtesies of golf and the rules of the game, you should be able to do the following:

1. List ten rules of etiquette which you think are most often violated as you play from tee to green.

2. List at least ten situations from which a player may gain relief without incurring a penalty.

3. Explain what is meant by "winter rules."

4. List at least five infringements of the rules for which a one-stroke penalty is awarded.

5. Describe the two situations which may be played under either the one-stroke or stroke-and-distance penalty.

6. Explain how a ball must be properly dropped.

7. List the four stroke-and-distance penalties and interpret how to count a penalty awarded under this category.

8. Define what is meant by a general penalty of golf.

9. List ten situations for which the general penalty of golf is awarded.

10. Explain the procedure which must be followed if you played into the cup with the wrong ball when playing stroke play.

11. Name five infringements of the rules for which you may be disqualified from a tournament.

Concept VII—Additional and More Suitable Equipment Will Eventually Become Necessary to Enhance Comfort and Expedite Progress

As YOU CONTINUE to golf you will want to secure the additional golf equipment which will aid you in improving your game. Perhaps it will even be advisable for you to change the type of ball and clubs you are using in order to realize your potential.

1. As your proficiency increases you will want to secure certain accessories which will add to the enjoyment of the game.

Although all of the items listed below are not absolutely necessary, they are usually part of the "wardrobe" of a golfer:

GLOVE. A full glove, worn on the left hand, is advisable to ensure a good grip. The extra money paid for the full glove will not be wasted.

SHOES. A pair of golf shoes with spiked soles is preferable to a shoe with any other kind of sole. A sound foundation is basic to a good golf swing, since your feet are your only contact with the ground. Your feet will not be nearly as apt to move and slip with golf shoes as with canvas or regular street shoes.

BAG. A bag larger than a "Sunday" bag will be required as you purchase more accessories and additional clubs. It is also important to have a pocket in the bag large enough for plastic rain gear and a sweater, as well as a holder for a golf umbrella.

CART. A "pull" cart may be desirable, since the bag will probably be quite heavy to carry. Carts of all types are available on a rental basis also. Some golfers prefer to employ a caddy or ride an electric cart.

RAIN GEAR. A golf umbrella will become an important item if one gets caught in the rain in the middle of a golf course. An umbrella, plastic raincoat and even golf rubbers will add much to one's comfort in inclement weather.

WARM CLOTHING. Since weather is changeable, a sweater or light jacket should be carried in the bag. Hand warmers are also useful when the weather is extremely cold.

TOWEL. A towel should be attached to the bag, as it is often needed to wipe off either hands or clubs when they become wet.

2. A complete set of matched clubs suited to your swing will facilitate your scoring potential.

As the golfer continues to practice and play the game, he will develop a "grooved" swing. In order not to have to change his swing to hit a "hard" 5 iron, when perhaps his basic swing with a 4 iron would be ideal, he should consider a full set of clubs similar to the set pictured earlier on page 9. The necessity to alter your swing will affect your timing and the "one basic swing" used for all normal full shots, so desirable in achieving success.

The addition of the sand wedge, with its increased loft, weight and more rounded flange, will help you hit through the sand when exploding a shot. A *dual wedge* is a club which is a combination of a pitching wedge and a sand wedge. Although usable for both pitch shots and explosion shots, it is better to have both a pitching wedge and a sand wedge.

It is very possible that you will have developed a much faster and stronger swing than you had as a beginner. If so, you might need a firmer shaft, with a correspondingly heavier swingweight, to achieve greater distance.

At this point check with your professional regarding your needs. It is usually possible to trade in your present set of clubs when purchasing another set. Perhaps he will also recommend that you switch to a higher-compression ball. Knowing you have the proper equipment will help your game immensely.

Outcomes

After reviewing the additional equipment suggested to aid you in improving your score and enhancing your comfort, you should be able to do the following:

1. List the various items of equipment considered as part of the "wardrobe" of the golfer who has passed beyond the state of a novice, and state the purpose of each item.

2. Discuss how your swing may change as you continue to play golf, and the implications these changes may have on the suitability of your equipment.

Concept VIII—Participation in a Pre-Season Conditioning Program and a Program of Maintenance During the Season, as Well as a Logical Method of Practicing Prior to Teeing-Off, Are Important Factors Related to Success in Golf

THOSE FORTUNATE ENOUGH to live in the warmer climates of the world usually do not consider a program of conditioning and maintenance quite as seriously as their northern neighbors. The opportunity to play golf on a year-round basis provides them with the finest and most natural method for maintenance. For the seasonal player and for anyone who wishes to improve his skill at the sport, a program of development *and* maintenance is essential.

1. A program of planned muscular development has proven successful to many top players.

Regardless of what type of program an individual undertakes, the objective is to strengthen those muscles which will aid him in striking the ball *harder with less effort*. This added strength not only increases the length of his drives, but results in smoother execution of the shorter shots. Better results are within the grasp of those who want to develop themselves.

There are many accepted programs to help you become stronger. Isotonic, isometric and general conditioning exercises are types which have proven extremely beneficial.

A) *ISOTONIC EXERCISE (WEIGHT TRAINING)*. This type of exercise involves moving a given amount of weight through a full range of motion. It is ideal to have bar bells and dumbbells with which to work; however, many home devices such as weighted boxes, sand-bags, chairs or bricks can be used as substitutes. In any case, start with weights that can be handled fairly easily, gradually adding more weight on a weekly basis. Following are a few excellent exercises that will increase strength in the muscles involved in hitting a golf ball: it is recommended that each exercise be repeated 30 times in groups (sets) of ten, and the program repeated three or four times a week.

1) *Wrist curls.* Sitting position, arms resting on thighs, and bar bell balanced firmly in hands. Curl wrists up and down. Do this with hands both above and below the bar.

2) *Upright rowing.* Standing position, arms in hanging position in front of body. Bar bell evenly balanced, hands together and over top of bar. Raise weight upward until hands touch chin, then lower to extended position once again.

3) *Knee bends.* Balance bar bell behind neck and on shoulders. Do *quarter* knee bends from standing position.

4) *Leg extensions.* Balance bar bell behind neck and on shoulders. Rise up on toes to full extension, then return to floor.

Wrist curls can also be done with dumbbells or a facsimile. Another excellent device is a wall pulley, useful to practice the golf swing with resistance. Work can be done to develop a good strong left arm, with pulling action from the left side.

Expanded programs involving the types of exercises mentioned above are commonly used by many high school and college golf teams today, as well as a great number of the "play-for-pay" golfers. The suggested workout, supplemented by hitting balls into a net, putting and a general conditioning exercise such as running, makes for a nicely rounded program and keeps the body in good tone.

B) *ISOMETRIC EXERCISE.* This kind of exercise involves a full contraction of a muscle or group of muscles without moving any weight. Following are some examples of this type of exercise: in each exercise, the exerted contraction time should be six to eight seconds.

1) Spread your fingers apart and press down on a table.

2) For forearm strength, hold a club with either hand about waist high and press it down against a table.

3) Press the club against a wall, using only the left-hand grip (as if hitting to a target). Assume just the right-hand grip and press the club against the wall toward the target.

Isometric exercise is good because it is simple to perform and no gadgets are needed. Exercises can be made up by the individual to fit his own neds. The effort exerted is not as measurable as the isotonic exercise. Each exercise must be given a maximum effort to receive the full benefit.

C) *GENERAL CONDITIONING.* Good muscle tone can be attained by following a daily program of exercise in varying degrees. A combination of weight-training, isometrics and general conditioning can be the most thorough program of development. Following are a few familiar exercises and activities that will help keep a person in good shape for golf: 1) Push-ups (on fingertips too); 2) Sit-ups; 3) Running; 4) Squats; 5) Jumping Jacks; 6) Waist-bends; 7) Handball or Paddleball; 8) Basketball; 9) Volleyball; 10) Badminton.

LEARNING EXPERIENCE—AN EXERCISE PROGRAM FOR YOU
Considering your own physical condition, the availability of equipment, a facility to work in, and any improvisation that you would like to make on your own, make up a good training program for golf that will work for you.

Before starting any intensive exercise program, you should have a *thorough physical check-up* and a clean bill of health from your physician. This is necessary so you will know how much stress you can put on your system.

2. Maintaining good physical condition and a sound golf swing is much simpler and less time-consuming than developing yourself physically.

Once a desirable physical level has been reached by an individual and the season begins, a very light daily program of exercise will keep your muscles in good tone. The recommended program of development has been centered around the *golf swing;* therefore, the key for maintenance is based on the same thing. A light program for each "off"-day can be most helpful for those who wish to be effective within their physical potential. Following is a list of prescribed exercises that can be used by a golfer once his active season of play has begun:

a) Use the "swing drill" exercises described in Concept IV.
b) Do a few push-ups.
c) Run in place for three minutes.
d) Swing a weighted club.
e) Do a few sit-ups and squats.
f) Perform two or three isometrics involving the arms and shoulders.

3. A logical method of practicing prior to teeing-off is most important.

It makes good sense to warm-up before playing a round of golf. Preceding participation in any competitive sport, there should be emphasis on loosening up and getting the muscles in proper tone for the contest. Whether exercises are done or golf shots are hit, the body is being prepared physically and mentally for the test that follows. Whenever possible, time should be allotted for this preparation. Many week-end players run to the first tee, waggle a club a few times and then tee the ball up. After swinging away at it, they watch it sail off to the right rough or duck-hook into the woods on the left. Turning to their playing partners they admit, "It wasn't very good, but I'm off the tee, it will take three or four holes to get it going." This kind of start can make for a long day, and can be avoided by warming-up properly. If a person arrives late at the first tee, he should at least step away from the teeing ground and take a number of full swings with his driver, starting slowly and finishing with a dozen vigorous full swings. This sets some kind of tempo. A recommended warm-up routine follows:

a) Start on the putting green. Begin with short putts of two and three feet, and move back gradually to longer ones. Concentrate on keeping still over the ball. Feel it!
b) Move to the practice hitting range, and start by loosening up with one or two swing drills followed by a few chip shots.
c) Begin hitting with the 8-iron (use the pitching wedge if there is one in the bag, then move to the 8-iron). Concentrate on firmness and smoothness, with about a three-quarter swing. Always hit toward a definite target.
d) Progress through the whole bag, using *every other* club, swinging full now, hitting four or five shots with each club

and finishing with the driver. This will gradually lengthen and strengthen the swing.

Watch the results of each shot and later, on the course, allow for any variation that happens to be in the swing on that given day. For example: if the ball was fading slightly to the right in practice, chances are that it will do the same thing later during the game. Use the swing that is with you that day, believe in it, and the day will be more enjoyable.

Outcomes

1. State the two factors that can be improved by a conditioning program.
2. Name the three types of conditioning programs recommended for golfers; explain how each is performed and the values of each.
3. Name and demonstrate four weight-training exercises for golfers.
4. Demonstrate three isometric exercises for golfers.
5. Name and demonstrate six calisthenics that will help keep one in shape for golf.
6. List four sports that can contribute to golf conditioning.
7. Name and demonstrate six activities that will contribute to the maintenance of physical condition for golf.
8. Explain the reasons for warming-up and practicing just before a round of golf.
9. List the steps you would follow in warming-up and practicing just before teeing-off for a round.

Concept IX—Golf's Origin Cannot Be Verified, But Its Early Acceptance Was Responsible for Its Rapid Growth and Development

France, Holland and Scotland each claim to have originated the game of golf. The French identify it with another game resembling golf played many centuries ago in France, while early Dutch paintings depict a game resembling golf played on ice. Numerous authorities, however, credit the origin of golf to the Scottish shepherds, who knocked pebbles into crude holes in the ground with their crooks—the game most resembling golf as it is played today. Regardless of which country originated the game, there are records available to prove that golf was played in Scotland during the 14th century.

Around 1440 golf's popularity began to spread. King James IV of Scotland became alarmed when he discovered that some of the Scottish people were spending more time practicing golf than archery. It was during this period that bows and arrows were used in warfare. In order to ensure the country's strength for war, Parliament declared golf illegal. Eventually the decree was ignored, when the king was discovered playing the game. Later, decrees were issued against the game because it offered too great a competition for church sermons. These later decrees did not stop the majority of the golf enthusiasts, however.

The first woman golfer mentioned by historians was Mary, Queen of Scotland. Queen Mary, who had received her education in France, referred to the boy who carried her clubs and served her on the golf course as her "cadet." The French pronunciation is "caddy," from which our term "caddie" is derived.

Courses of various lengths were being set up everywhere. In 1754 the Royal and Ancient Golf Club of St. Andrews in Scotland was founded. This course is still considered to be the world shrine of golfdom and one of the most outstanding courses in the world today. It is considered the birthplace of modern golf. Early courses consisted of various numbers of holes, and rounds of different lengths were played. St. Andrews happened to have nine holes which were played "out," and the same nine holes were used to play "in." Soon the 18-hole round became the established practice. It was at the St. Andrews Golf Club in 1754 that a committee formulated the first set of rules to govern the game of golf. There were 13 rules in number, almost all of which still remain in existence today.

The British Open, inaugurated in 1860, is the oldest established permanent golf championship in the world. This tournament was referred to as the Open to emphasize that it was an official tournament open to all professionals, regardless of where they lived or with what club they were affiliated. In 1861 amateurs were also declared eligible for the Open. Thus the true meaning of the word *open* (a competition for both pros and amateurs) was in existence. The British Open is the only major championship held annually outside the United States. It was at this Open that the present-day format of 72 holes of stroke play was inaugurated. Formerly this tournament consisted of only 36 holes.

The introduction of golf in America came via Scottish settlers. As early as 1733 there were some references made to golf societies in the United States. The St. Andrews Society founded in this country devoted itself to the renewal of Scottish golf customs.

It was in 1888 that John G. Reid, a Scotsman, called the "Father of American Golf," along with four other men, formed the first golf club in the United States. The club established in Yonkers, New York was named St. Andrews. The failure to obtain a lease from the owner of the cow pasture used for the golf club soon forced the group to move to another site. The first permanent course with a clubhouse was built at the Shinnecock Hills Golf Course in Westchester County, New York.

It soon became necessary to have a central governing body responsible for the conduct of the sport and the numerous competitions that were being planned. In 1894, a committee from five private clubs met and founded the United States Golf Association. The U.S. Amateur, U.S. Open and Women's Championships were first played in 1895. Rules were set down by the

USGA to govern play in these championships. From this period on, the USGA became the governing body of golf in this country.

Professional golfers did not have an organization of their own until 1916. Rodman Wanamaker was the leader responsible for the formation of the Professional Golfers Association (PGA) on April 10, 1916. The establishment of the Ladies Professional Golf Association (LPGA), its sister organization, soon followed. These two organizations are responsible for numerous regulations governing professional tournaments.

In 1936, The National Golf Foundation was organized by the leading manufacturers of golfing equipment as a non-profit agency whose main purpose was to encourage participation in golf, and to provide information on all matters pertaining to the golf course. Presently this organization also furnishes service and information on the instructional aspects of the game.

Since 1965, the Lifetime Sports Education Project, a project of the American Association for Health, Physical Education and Recreation, has also done much to stimulate the teaching of golf —along with numerous other lifetime sports—in the schools of the nation. Their clinicians have conducted classes for selected golf teachers throughout the nation, offering them ideas for teaching large groups in limited facilities with little equipment. These teachers then conduct similar sessions for the other golf teachers in the districts of their respective states, thus "snowballing" the movement toward improved instruction.

1. The improvements in golf equipment have had a decided effect on the golf scores of the present day.

Probably the greatest achievement that any amateur can attain is the "Grand Slam" of golf, consisting of winning in the same year the British Open, U.S. Open, British Amateur and U.S. Amateur. Bobby Jones achieved this feat in 1930. Some of the great analysts of the game agree that golfers are no better today than they were in the era of Bobby Jones; it is primarily the *equipment* that has altered the scores.

Around 1618 the golf ball maker for King James VI was making the balls of wood. Between this period and 1848, leather-covered balls stuffed with boiled goose feathers became the most popular golf ball. A good ball maker could make about four of these balls in a day. The balls were not perfectly round and became soggy in wet weather. Most of the clubheads at this time were wooden, as iron clubs caused too much wear on the balls.

Gutta percha balls were introduced in the mid-19th century and caused significant changes in the game. The "gutties" were made by hand-rolling the gutta percha on a flat board. The material was softened in hot water and then shaped. To get truer flight, indented surfaces in iron molds were used. Iron clubs increased, due to the tougher ball, and hickory replaced the ash shafts. In 1894 A. G. Spalding & Bros., Inc. hired some Scottish club makers and made the first American clubs. Around 1898 the desire to hit a longer ball initiated Coburn Haskell, associated with the B. F. Goodrich Co., to introduce a rubber ball. From that time on more specific regulations regarding size, weight and other factors regarding changes in balls and clubs became necessary. In 1924 the USGA approved the steel shaft. Recently the aluminum shaft has also gained acceptance. Around 1930 the wooden tee replaced the mound of sand on which the ball was placed. The R and A and the USGA have attempted, through the ages, to preserve the original form of the game and have been quite successful in achieving this end. However, companies can continue to improve their clubs and balls, as long as they conform to the rules. Nowhere does the USGA attempt to regulate the raw materials used to improve the equipment.

2. Golf is the fastest growing competitive sport in the United States today.

People of all ages, engaged in nearly every occupation and including many retired individuals, enjoy the game of golf universally. It would be impossible to know exactly how many million people in the world are participating in this sport today.

In the United States, the National Golf Foundation conducts nationwide studies on almost every conceivable phase of the growth of the game and the courses on which it is played. The period from 1950 to the present has seen the greatest increase of people playing the game, a number more than doubling the previous estimate. The NGF estimates for 1968 indicated that over nine million people in the United States played golf, and had approximately 9336 golf course facilities on which to play. In 1945, approximately 4800 courses were available. The golf equipment sales increased to over $150 million a year. In the period from 1958 to 1967 these sales more than doubled. These statistics should be sufficient evidence that golf is presently the nation's fastest growing competitive sport.

The NGF cites numerous reasons for the popularity of golf in the United States. They recognize that, due to the increase of leisure time and a rise of wages in industry, more individuals of average income now play the game. Television is also exposing millions of people to the game.

Schools and communities, introducing golf to the junior set, have contributed greatly to the increase. The stress on the life-time value of the sport has interested a number of retired people. These are but a few of the reasons golf is so popular today.

Outcomes

After studying the history of golf, you should be able to:

1. Discuss the early laws which made the playing of golf illegal, and give the reasons for their enactment.

2. Name the course at which the 18-hole round was established, and explain how this number was selected.

3. Explain what is meant by an "Open" tournament.

4. Discuss the introduction of the game of golf in the United States, and name the person most responsible for its acceptance.

5. List the various organizations which sprang up in the United States since 1894 to govern or promote the game of golf, and state briefly the purposes of each.

6. State what is meant by the "Grand Slam" of golf, and tell who achieved this feat.

7. Describe the various types of balls and clubs used from 1618 to the present.

8. Discuss the growth of the game of golf in the United States as shown by the NGF studies, and list several reasons for its increasing popularity.

Concept X—A Golfer Should Never Stop Searching for Additional Information Which Will Aid Him in Mastering the Various Aspects of the Game of Golf

LISTED BELOW ARE some selected references which will aid you in continuing to learn more about the game of golf:

Bibliography

1. Armour, Tommy. *How to Play Your Best Golf All the Time.* Greenwich, Conn.: Fawcett Publications, Inc., 1953.

2. Hahn, Paul. *Paul Hahn Shows You How to Play Trouble Shots.* N.Y.: David McKay Co., Inc., 1965.

3. Player, Gary. *Gary Player's Golf Secrets.* Englewood Cliffs, N.J.: Prentice-Hall, Inc., 1962.

4. Palmer, Arnold. *My Game and Yours.* N.Y.: Simon and Schuster, Inc., 1963.

5. Nicklaus, Jack. *My 55 Ways to Lower Your Golf Score.* N.Y.: Simon and Schuster, Inc., 1962.

6. Jacobs, John. *Golf by John Jacobs.* London: Stanley Paul and Co. Ltd., 1963.

7. Jones, Robert Tyre. *Bobby Jones on Golf.* Garden City, N.Y.: Doubleday and Co., Inc., 1966.

8. Burke, Jack Jr., Nelson, Byron, Revolta, Johnny, Runyan, Paul and Smith, Horton. *How to Solve Your Golf Problems.*

9. Berg, Patty and Dypwick, Otis. *Golf.* N.Y.: A. S. Barnes and Co., 1941.

10. Wright, Mickey. *Play Golf the Wright Way.* Garden City, N.Y.: Doubleday and Co., Inc., 1962.

11. Flaherty, Tom. *The U.S. Open: 1895/1965*. N.Y.: E. P. Dutton and Co., Inc., 1966.

12. *Golf Course Growth in the United States*. The National Golf Foundation, 1967.

13. *The Rules of Golf*. The United States Golf Association, current.

MAGAZINES

Golf. New York, N.Y. Universal Publishing and Distributing Corp.

Golf Digest. Norwalk, Conn. Golf Digest, Inc.

Golf World. Southern Pines, N.C. Golf World Co., Inc.

THERE IS NO SUBSTITUTE, HOWEVER, FOR A VISIT TO A TRAINED, EXPERIENCED GOLF PROFESSIONAL.

1K1995